Why Your
Business Sucks

Here's What To Do When Your Business Is
Driving You Crazy, Wearing You Down, And
Burning You Out

Mike Agugliaro

ISBN-13: 978-1540595003
ISBN-10: 1540595005

DEDICATION

To Rob Zadotti – a great friend and business partner, who stuck with me through all my crazy ways. **We're just getting started!**

CONTENTS

WARRIOR WARNINGS — p 6

DOES YOUR BUSINESS SUCK? — p.7

HERE'S WHY YOUR BUSINESS MIGHT SUCK — p.8

WHY YOUR BUSINESS SUCKS #1: YOU ARE BURNED OUT, FED UP AND FRUSTRATED BY EVERYTHING AND YOU'RE READY TO THROW IN THE TOWEL, SELL THE BUSINESS, AND MAYBE GO BACK TO WORKING FOR SOMEONE ELSE — p.15

WHY YOUR BUSINESS SUCKS #2: MONEY IS TIGHT AND IT'S A STRUGGLE TO MAKE PAYROLL — p.22

WHY YOUR BUSINESS SUCKS #3: THE WAY YOU WERE TAUGHT TO LEAD IS ALL WRONG — p.27

WHY YOUR BUSINESS SUCKS #4: YOU WERE NEVER TAUGHT HOW TO BUILD A STRATEGIC PLAN — p.33

WHY YOUR BUSINES SUCKS #5: YOUR COMPETITORS SEEM TO BE HIRING ALL THE GOOD PEOPLE — p.38

WHY YOUR BUSINESS SUCKS #6: WHY YOUR RECRUITING AND HIRING SUCKS — p.42

WHY YOUR BUSINESS SUCKS #7: YOUR TEAM IS NOT PRODUCTIVE AND THEY JUST END UP DOING THEIR OWN THING — p.48

WHY YOUR BUSINESS SUCKS #8: YOUR   p.52
CUSTOMERS HAVE NO LOYALTY –
THEY JUST CALL THE FIRST COMPANY
THEY THINK OF… AND IT'S NOT
ALWAYS YOU

WHY YOUR BUSINESS SUCKS #9: YOUR   p.58
BRAND IS WEAK

WHY YOUR BUSINESS SUCKS #10:   p.63
YOUR MARKETING ISN'T DELIVERING
THE LEADS YOU NEED

BONUS CHAPTER: MAYBE YOU WANT   p.69
YOUR BUSINESS TO SUCK???

SPECIAL REPORT: NETWORKING   p.74
YOUR WAY TO BROKE

SPECIAL REPORT: HOW TO GET A   p.84
VENDOR TO PAY YOU TO IMPROVE
YOUR BUSINESS

HERE'S YOUR ACTION PLAN   p.88

YOU CAN DO THIS – TAKE THE LEAP   p.91
NOW

ADDITIONAL RESOURCES AND   p.92
STRATEGIES FROM MIKE AUGUGLIARO

WARRIOR WARNINGS

Do you feel frustrated in your business?

Do your employees drive you nuts and need a lot of hand-holding and follow-up to make sure they do what they're supposed to do?

Do you spend money with few results?

Do you keep spending money on the same things even though you're not getting the results... just because you don't have any other options?

Do you struggle to make payroll?

Do you wish you could hire great employees?

Do you, personally, spend too much time at your office instead of being at home with your family?

Did things turn out differently in your business than you were expecting them to when you first started?

If you answered "yes" to some or all of these questions, you're not alone. Many service business owners just like you face the same frustrations daily. Unfortunately, if you answered "yes" to any of these questions then you should take that as a warning that your business is in jeopardy.

Maybe it's not going to fold tomorrow, next week, or even next year, but your business is at very serious risk – you could lose money, become unprofitable, and even burn out.

Answering yes to any of these questions is a warning sign to you – that your business is at risk. Fortunately, the strategies you learn in this book can help you change that around.

I did it in my own business when my business partner and I realized that we were burning out and our business sucked. And I show people how to do the same thing I did – to turn around their businesses and create the business and life they want and deserve.

Keep reading to find out how to fix these problems in your business...

DOES YOUR BUSINESS SUCK?

If you feel that your business sucks right now – either because it's burning you out or because you've reached a plateau, I've got some good news for you…

You can change things around.

I've done it and I'll show you how.

Step by step, piece by piece, let's roll up our sleeves and work together. That's how I rebuilt my business from a struggling business to a $30+ million a year business…

… That's how I've helped hundreds of other service businesses all over the world…

… And that's how I'd like to help YOU in YOUR business.

If you feel that your business sucks, it can change.

<u>Starting now.</u>

Turn the page and let's begin…

HERE'S WHY YOUR BUSINESS MIGHT SUCK

Your service business sucks.

There, I said it.

Your service business sucks (or at least it feels that way sometimes). Maybe you're frustrated by the daily challenges and difficulties and you're thinking of throwing in the towel. Or maybe your service business is actually a success but you sometimes feel like it sucks because you've hit a plateau or it's not growing as fast as you want.

I've faced ALL those situations. I've been there! No matter the reason, you feel it: your service business sucks.

I'm not saying this to be cruel but actually to help you. As I always say, "I'd rather hear a hurtful truth than a comforting lie" and that's why I wrote this book: to cut through the noise and the BS that's out there, and then to call out the challenges you're facing so we can create a plan to help you build an amazing business.

Look, some books will try to walk lightly over the topic and tell you things you want to hear before they try to sneak in their main point. They'll pretend to be kind by saying "oh, your business is amazing and here's how to make it even better."

That's not me. If you hang around my world for very long, you're going to learn something that shocks some people: I get right to the point and fearlessly tackle the difficult reality. While other people soften their words because they think they're being kind, I believe I'm providing the real kindness by just saying it like it is.

Your service business sucks. That's the way it is. **Fortunately, that's not the way it has to be. In this book, we're going to roll up our sleeves and work together to put you on a path toward creating the kind of business you originally wanted to start.**

Maybe you're wondering what gives me the right to say your service business sucks, or how I can make some recommendations to help you turn things around. Good question (and you should be asking this of anyone you learn from, or any industry group or association you become part of!)

Just over 22 years ago, my business partner Rob Zadotti and I started Gold Medal Electric. We were young, energetic, passionate, and we were certain we had what it took to become successful.

Our business sucked. At first it was fun: we did what we needed to do to build our business. We worked 24/7, the way most start-ups do. But thing is: it never got better. We worked HARD, daily, grinding it out all over the state to serve any customer we could find. Those 24/7 start-up days never ended and a decade later we were still two guys in two vans, with a couple of helpers, working our butts off… missing family time, working from before sunrise to well after sunset, tip-toeing home each night so we didn't wake our spouses (or worse: face the lie about what time I said I would be home).

This lasted for one very rough decade. And then one day my business partner came to me and said he was nearly burned out and he was out. I thought he meant he was out for the day… He meant he was out forever.

It was a shock, yet at the same time it was not a shock at all because I was on the verge of burning out too. But I knew I couldn't continue by myself because I would burn out even faster.

Instead of shutting everything down, **we realized there was another way: we decided to change the game and transform our business and build a business the way we knew it could become. We were ready to jump off a cliff and either land as a successful business… Or die trying. We got brave.**

We invested more than $900,000 in our education. Yes, I know that amount of money sounds crazy but we needed a solution. We realized that kids go to college for $250,000; so we created our own "college" education. We even went outside of the service business industry to look at what other companies were doing – like Amazon, Disney, Zappos, and 1-800-GOT-JUNK. We pulled together the best ideas and strategies from everywhere we could find and we rebuilt our business.

Gold Medal Electric became Gold Medal Service and our two barely-running old vans were replaced by a growing fleet of beautiful yellow and black trucks. And, we started hiring, focusing on top performers who could help us grow.

The first decade sucked. The second decade was very different: we grew every single year, and our revenue increased by a minimum of a million each year (usually more) and are on track to earn more than $30+ million this year. We serve more than 125,000 customers all over New Jersey. We have a team of more than 190 people and we are in constant hiring mode. We have 140 fleet on the road. We have a 15,000 square foot building and just acquired another 10,000 square foot building because our growth trajectory is climbing so quickly that we need to expand *yesterday*.

Perhaps more important for you: my business partner and I continue to own and run our business but we have now built a business that we have bene able to own and run without dealing with the day-to-day stuff any longer. In fact, we no longer have offices at our head office. Yes, I still go there and yes I still make sure things are on track and yes I still deal with issues now and then... but I have a very strong and capable team that deals with the day-to-day stuff. That means I can focus on growing my business and even take vacations with my wife and kids.

I'm not telling you this to boast but rather to show you a couple of things:

First, that service businesses do suck.

Second, that service businesses can be turned around – and the results can be amazing.

Third, that I studied how to do it and now I help other service business owners do the same thing – transform their struggling companies into successful businesses that ultimately reward the service business owners.

Fourth, I want to show you how to turn your business around – to take it from sucking to successful.

If your business is experiencing the pain and struggle that I did in my first decade of business, let me show you how to get out of that and put yourself into a position to start enjoying the amazing growth like my second decade.

This book is laser-focused on some of the big issues that many service business owners experience when their business sucks. The things you'll read in this book won't comprehensively cover everything that could go wrong but should give you some really practical ideas to help you make changes to get things going in the right direction.

I haven't been to college. I'm a graduate of a vocational trade school and I've been on my own since I was very young. I've been figuring it out as I go, attending the school of daily learning and action, and discovering (often through trial and error) how to create the life that I want. I did it and I want to show you how you can do it too.

I'm not here to sell you anything. That's the reason that most people come and see me... they know I'll deliver straight talk with zero sales pitches. I'm here to serve you.

Let's start with this: **Why did you get into the service business to begin with?**

In general I meet service business owners who typically started their business for one of the following reasons:

- Maybe the business is a family business that was passed down to you. You took the reins and started working at it but you realize that this multi-generational business has some challenges and you're stuck between a rock and a hard place while you try to work through those challenges yet maintain the status quo.

- Or, maybe you got into the trades and at first you started working for someone else but then realized that you could probably do a better job than the company you were working for. So you branched out on your own. Some days you might be happier… But there are probably some days where you'd like to pack it in and just go back to being an employee.
- Or, maybe owning your own service business was always the path you envisioned because of the wealth and freedom it would provide you. How's that working out for you? Are you getting the wealth and freedom you were hoping for?

You probably started your service business for one or more of those reasons. And, if you're anything like the other service business owners I meet, you're probably discovering that running a service business is a significant challenge.

Today's service businesses are more complex than ever. The truth is: It's hard to run a service business successfully, profitably, with a good loyal team in today's changing environment.

- People's buying habits are changing.
- Online marketing allows all your competitors to get ultra-aggressive in their marketing (and maybe even it's hard to compete ethically when your competitors are getting unethical in the marketing they do!)
- Social media gives complainers a platform.
- Employees don't seem as dedicated or motivated as you were when you started in the business.
- Costs are rising faster than you can raise your prices.
- … and I'm probably just scratching the surface of the challenges you face day-in and day-out.

That's the reality. You know that's the reality already and if you're reading this book, maybe you're already struggling and fighting against that reality. So, what can be done about it?

You could press on in frustration, not knowing what to do about it and just accepting that this is the way it's going to be from now on. That's not ideal and, if you choose to do that, you WILL burn out. Maybe not this year or next but at some point that negativity and all the hardship will take its toll on your physical, mental, and emotional wellbeing. It will wreck you and your relationships.

Or, you could bitch and whine and complain and moan and grumble to anyone who listens. Believe me, I know there are plenty of service business owners who do that! (Chances are, that's NOT you... since I've found that people who choose to read this book fall into some of the latter categories that I'm about to explain)...

Or, could do what I did and decide to do something about it. **You accept that times are changing and you step up to change with the times. You admit that you don't know everything and you're willing to try anything that makes sense. You roll up your sleeves and dig in. You put yourself around other people who are farther down the road than you, who you can model yourself after and even get mentored by. You invest in yourself and your education to learn what you need to know, and you start implementing daily and hourly to make massive, positive changes in your business.**

If you're reading this book, I'm pretty sure you're like that third person – the one willing to step up and take responsibility. After all, it's not just about you! Your family depend on you, your employees depend on your, and your customers depend on you. You have a lot of people who believe that you can and will do something to turn things around and to transform your business from sucking to skyrocketing. Maintain that attitude, keep searching out the answers, and keep pushing yourself to try things (even if you're scared) and you can discover what I discovered: that change and growth are possible.

Here's the good news: **there are service businesses out there right now that are thriving because they've discovered how to succeed even in this changing market.**

- No matter the size of the business or the market they work in
- No matter what markets they work in, or even what country they operate in
- No matter what other competitors are present in their market
- No matter how "broken" the owner thinks the business might be

... There are businesses that have overcome the kinds of challenges you're facing and now they are growing and succeeding right now.

If you're not happy with where your business is (and even if you've just come to tolerate the way it is), or if you just want to get more out of your business so you can have the life you want, then let me ask you this question: What do you want your service business to be like?

Let's start with that fundamental question. If you don't know what you want your service business to be like – if you don't have something you prefer – then you might as well throw this book out now and do something else because this book will not help you. You need a vision for what you want to accomplish. Then, and only then, will you be able to move forward... **in the direction of that vision.**

Take Action!

At this point, I'm sure you know things have to change and you're ready to start your own education (just like my business partner and I started ours). To help you extract all the value and strategies you can from this book, I've included these *Take Action* sections throughout the book. Each *Take Action* section includes (1) a few recommended actions that are specific to the chapter, and (2), an area where you can list Stop Doing actions, Keep Doing actions, and Start Doing actions.

Recommended actions:

___ Think about this question and answer it honestly: why did you start your service business?

_____

_____

___ What are the frustrations you face in your business today?

_____

_____

___ What do you wish your service business could be like?

_____

_____

Review the following and add your own actions to stop doing, keep doing, or start doing, as well as who will do them and by when:

___ Stop doing actions (Actions you currently do now but should stop doing)

_____

_____

__ Keep doing actions (Actions you currently do now and should keep doing)

_____

_____

__ Start doing actions (Actions you don't do now but should start doing)

_____

_____

"Powerful transformation begins in your life and business the moment you decide to make a change."

-Mike Agugliaro

Get the latest strategies for free at CEOWARRIOR.com…

WARRIOR POWER

"I just wanted to let you guys know how incredible last week was. You are masters of creating experiences. The content was amazing. I had more fun than the June 2015 event, which I didn't think was possible. I am going into 2016 more prepared than I've ever been for any year. Also, I am truly honored to be a part of your group. You have instilled a level of confidence and certainty in me that I cannot explain. I know you've probably heard this from a lot of other people. You've changed my life."

Brian Vardiman 2nd Year Warrior

WHY YOUR BUSINESS SUCKS #1: YOU ARE BURNED OUT, FED UP AND FRUSTRATED BY EVERYTHING AND YOU'RE READY TO THROW IN THE TOWEL, SELL THE BUSINESS, AND MAYBE GO BACK TO WORKING FOR SOMEONE ELSE

When was the last time you took a vacation?

(And when I say "vacation" I mean a vacation when you're not worried about your business so you're phoning and texting every day!)

When was the last time you got to spend some really quality time with your family... without having a nagging feeling in your gut about a problem at the office?

When was the last time you and your spouse went on a romantic getaway together... because you had the time, the energy, the money, and no pressing emergencies in your service business?

In my first ten years of running my service business, I struggled to have any of those things. I barely made it to my son's birth; and even while my amazing wife/Goddess, Jennifer (who was going through labor) understood my struggles and asked me how work that day! She knew how hard I worked for our family, and how much I wanted my business to succeed even though it was a constant grind.

When my business partner came to me and told me that he was burning out and was thinking about leaving, I thought briefly about shutting down the business and going to work for someone else. It seemed to make sense – there were fewer problems and, when you compared the expenses I was paying and the time I was on the road, I felt like I could make more money pushing shopping carts.

And maybe that's exactly where you are right now… Frustrated, nearly burning out, and wondering what you should do next… And maybe very tempted to pack it all in and go back to working for someone else – if for no other reason than to be able to take vacations again or to be able to go home at the end of the day with fewer worries.

I've been there, but I urge you to keep reading this chapter because I want to share with you some insight with you:

You need to know that a struggling service business is not doomed to failure. You can turn it around. I've done it and I've showed many other service business owners *all over the world* how to do it too.

It all starts with your MINDSET… deciding what you want and then making that picture clear in your mind.

Unfortunately, what happens with many service business owners, is that they may start their business with an optimistic mindset but they soon get frustrated and overwhelmed and even angry at how things are going. Then they begin to feel that "the struggle" is their reality. Everything gets defined around that struggle and hardship. Soon, their very identity is one of fighting a losing battle.

Have you ever known someone who, quite frankly, loved being sick? Every time you talk to them they're suffering from some other ailment or illness. It might just be a cold or allergies or headaches. But every single time you ask them how they are, they talk about their poor health. Or, if it's not their own health, it's the bad health of someone they know. I think we all know someone like that. They define their entire world around their bad health and soon even the slightest thing reinforces that belief.

The same thing happens to service business owners. A few annoyances and struggles that happen in every business soon begins to define their entire reality. Then, even the smallest speedbump reinforces what you believe about your business.

Now let's talk about how you could, should, and perhaps once DID envision your business… Not as a "sick", frustrating business but as a **healthy, vibrant, booming business…**

Every service business owner envisions their business in a certain way. Maybe you dream of a business that runs smoothly so you don't have to try and "put out fires" every single day. Or maybe you dream of a business in which the employees step up as proactive and hard-working "team members". Or maybe you dream of a business that is actually so profitable that it's no problem making payroll every week. Or maybe you dream of a business that actually allows you to take home a wage that grows each year and allows you to treat your family to the lifestyle you want to give them.

Every service business owner will dream something slightly different but I like to summarize all these dreams with three terms: wealth, freedom, and market domination.

In my mind, these three words perfectly summarize what every service business COULD and SHOULD be. Yes, you might define the exact numbers behind these words differently but these three terms are central to what you probably envision for your business.

Wealth

When we hear the word "wealth" we tend to think of financial wealth and certainly that's a big component of what I'm talking about. My vision for all the service business owners I meet is to help them **achieve substantial financial wealth**. But even financial wealth is open to interpretation: is it a specific number in the bank? Is it a specific monthly income for their business? Is it a specific monthly income for their family? Is it having zero debt? Is it having a certain amount of net worth? Is it having no worries about retirement? As you can see, wealth is a wide-open concept.

Even beyond financial wealth, you might also note that we are wealthy in other ways: **you might have a large network of people** (perhaps you've heard the saying that "your network is your net worth.") And, we can be **wealthy in terms of our opportunities** – someone with a lot of options might be said to be wealthier than someone who has no options.

Freedom

Like wealth, "freedom" is open to interpretation as well. I like to think of it primarily as **the ability to do what you want when you want, without any worries of time or money**… not in the sense of anarchy but in the sense of having your life built in such a way that you can step back from the responsibilities of your business to spend a week with your spouse... while your business continues running on its own. If you can leave for a week or even a month, and get back to your business with little impact (or even better results!) then you have freedom. But if you leave for a week and everything falls apart then you do not have freedom.

But freedom extends beyond that to other areas, too: for example, the **health freedom** to be able to live the life you want. Maybe you have the **business freedom** I mentioned above but if you are stuck in a hospital bed then do you really have freedom? Or if you want to be healthy but are addicted to cigarettes or bad food choices, do you really have freedom? **Freedom is your ability to choose, so how much choice do you have?**

Market Domination

Most people understand wealth and freedom to some degree but not everyone understands market domination. And, in fact, some even say, "well I don't want to run a national home service business; I just want to run a business in my little market." However, market domination is not about being the absolute BIGGEST in the world or even in your state or market. Rather, **market domination is about being the absolute BEST choice** for your specific avatar... the ONLY company that your target market calls when they need service. And why wouldn't you want to be that for your customers?

You Can Have Wealth, Freedom, And Market Domination In Your Business

You might have taken offense earlier in this book when I said "your service business sucks." I didn't do that to make you mad at me; rather, I did that to shed a dramatic light on the disconnect between your vision for what you want your business to be like but the day-to-day reality of what your business is.

The truth is: I don't want your service business to suck because that means you show up every day to a service business that is not fulfilling to you and does not serve your family. I want you to own a business that fulfills you and serves your family and gives you the life you want.

We can help you get there together. It starts with your clear vision of what your business could be and of the wealth, freedom, and market domination that you want. And now, for the rest of the book, we'll start you on the path toward achieving that wealth, freedom, and market domination.

Take a moment to reflect on what wealth, freedom, and market domination could mean for you based on what I've explained here, and consider how you define each one and envision what the perfect level of wealth, freedom, and market domination mean for you. Then use these definitions to help you make decisions in your business.

I have a team of Master Coach Trainers and we work together to help service businesses all over the world break free from the mindset that their business is frustrating, and break free from the myths of sales and marketing that are repeated over and over, and then rebuild a new mindset of making strategic moves daily to achieve wealth, freedom, and market domination in whatever market or trade-line(s) you work in.

And we also believe in the importance of helping our fellow service business owners (because I KNOW the struggle you're facing). **That's why we regularly schedule time for a free, 30 minute one-on-one strategy call with any service business owner that wants to connect with us and get our help with a strategy, problem, question, or opportunity that needs clarity and direction.** On every call one of our Master Coach Trainers will work through whatever problem you have and help you put together a hands-on plan to fix it. The call is totally free and no, there's no hard selling tactics. (If you hang around with me long enough you'll know that I don't like that kind of cheesy approach to business.) Instead, we'll just help you put together a rock-solid strategy to deal with whatever situation you want to talk about – about how to address it and implement it, and what other educational options might be available to help you take further action and grow your business. **Schedule your free 30 minute strategy call with a Master Coach Trainer at: www.warriortoday.com**

Take Action!

Recommended actions:

___ What do you want wealth to look like?

_____

_____

__ What do you want freedom to look like?

_____

_____

__ What do you want market domination to look like?

_____

_____

__ Describe your ideal business (what you want your business to become).

_____

_____

__ **Schedule your free 30 minute strategy call with a Master Coach Trainer at www.warriortoday.com**

Add your own actions:

__ Stop doing actions (Actions you currently do now but should stop doing)

_____

_____

__ Keep doing actions (Actions you currently do now and should keep doing)

_____

_____

___ Start doing actions (Actions you don't do now but should start doing)

_____

_____

STOP. *Did you fill in the section above?* **I want you to get as much as you can out of this book.** *I know that going through this process will have a powerful effect on your business so make sure you complete all the steps. (Never skim or skip a step… as I always say, "How you do anything is how you do everything.")*

"Average action gets average results. Extraordinary action gets extraordinary results. What kind of results you want should determine the kind of action to take. So, what kind of results do you want?"

-Mike Agugliaro

Get the latest strategies for free at <u>CEOWARRIOR.com</u>…

21

WARRIOR POWER

"Being a Warrior in the CEO Warrior Circle is like running with a pack of wolves -- I'm part of an elite brotherhood that strives to be the best and dominate the market. The coaching, mentorship, motivation, and accountability are all so valuable. Mike is willing to serve! We get to see how everything works in real time because Mike teaches what he's actually doing and what's proven. And, the blueprint allows us to implement faster than we could do on our own. Since joining, we've seen 40% growth -- and that's just in one trade! We've also seen improvements in marketing, in team performance, in team morale, and in our ability to serve our clients better."

Darrin Gilmore

WHY YOUR SERVICE BUSINESS SUCKS #2: MONEY IS TIGHT AND IT'S A STRUGGLE TO MAKE PAYROLL

Lack of money in a service business – it's a common problem. It's common… and it's devastating!

It's devastating to you, the business owner (of course) because you put so much of yourself into your business. It's devastating to your employees because they rely on you and trust that you'll be able to give them a paycheck so they can provide for their families. It's also devastating to your customers and the community because home services is an important service and a contributor to the health and safety of your customers and their families.

There are several reasons why money might be tight but it all comes down to how much money your company earns. **When it comes to your company's financials, your job as a service business owner is to make more money and to become more profitable.**

If you start implementing some of the strategies I talk about in the this book, you should start to see some financial changes as well. For example, a strong brand, with highly-focused marketing, and backed up with a framework of service, is a very powerful way to generate more business. It's how I grew my business from struggling for a decade (struggling even to make six figures a year)... then I implemented these and other strategies, and the next decade was so different: our revenue grew by more than a million each year. In fact, I'm on track to make over $30 million this year.

So, why do some service businesses struggle while other succeed? **It all comes down to how well you can get your customers to buy from you.** I'm not talking about aggressive and shady sales practices. That doesn't serve your customers at all. Rather, you need to **provide high value in all of your products and services, and you need to serve your customers at the highest level to help them invest in the products or services that are right for them.**

And, when your customers pay you, how is that money managed? You also need an understanding of basic money strategies. When I hold my Warrior Fast Track Academy events, I spend some time making sure my audience has the understanding and strategies they need to manage their money wisely, which ensures more revenue and profit. Do you have a coach or mentor who can show you how to do this in your business?

Do You Have A Cross-Pollination Strategy?

Many service business owners sell one thing to one customer and then move on. But that customer rarely only ever needs one thing; they need additional services and products over the years.

For example, if you sell electrical services, your customers might hire you to wire in their newly renovated kitchen. Great. Once you're done that, apply a cross-pollination strategy and sell them other services and products that are relevant to them.

- You might point out that they could benefit from a surge protector installed in their home to keep their valuable electronics safe from power surges.
- You might offer them a generator to ensure that their power remains constant even during bad weather – especially to preserve the food in their fridge and freezer.
- You might point out that people who renovate their kitchen will also frequently follow it up with a bathroom renovation, and you can offer to rewire their bathroom... or... you could sell them one day bathroom solutions (which might provided by you, or which you have a referral agreement in place with a local one day bath

solutions company – so you get paid for the referral even though you don't do the work).

Cross-pollination is all about offering customers what they want, and then following it up with other products and services that they need.

Get creative about identifying what might help your customers the most. One way to do this is to make a list of the services and products you sell (or have a referral agreement in place) and identify what people often buy after they've bought the first time. List 2-3 cross-pollination services/products for everything that you sell. That way, you'll always have something to offer your customers.

We cover this in detail during my 4-day Warrior Fast Track Academy. Take the time learn how to do this, or show up to my event and get the fast, effective "short cut" to put this plan into motion in your company.

Do You Have A Follow-Up Strategy?

Cross-pollination doesn't just happen once when you're providing the customer with an estimate and discussing the project. Cross-pollination happens later, too. Once you've finished the first project, you can offer the second. Or call them back a couple weeks later and see if they're interested. Then follow up by email with another offer. Then follow up later with a direct mail package. And again by phone.

Find reasons to contact your customers and, once you have their attention, offer them something. Here are some reasons to contact your customers:

- Following-up about the project a month later to make sure it's performing for them.
- Following-up 3-6 months later as a check-in on the larger projects you completed for them.
- Contacting them to let them know that there's a major storm moving into the area and to keep their family safe.
- Reminding them about daylight savings time, and that they should move their clocks forward or back.
- Telling them that someone else in the neighborhood purchased a product or service and you think your customer might benefit from the same product or service.
- When you have a new package – such as a seasonal special.

Your customers will buy from you when you provide them with amazing value and service, and help them to see how your offers can help them keep their family safe and comfortable.

There are so many other ways to increase your revenue. If you'd like to explore this further in your business, then book your free 30 minute strategy call with a Master Coach Trainer at: www.warriortoday.com

Take Action!

Recommended actions:

__ What money issues do you deal with?

_____

_____

__ What are the frustrations you face with your money today?

_____

_____

__ What do you wish your business's wealth could be like?

_____

_____

__ Schedule your free 30 minute strategy call with a Master Coach Trainer at www.warriortoday.com

Add your own actions:

___ Stop doing actions (Actions you currently do now but should stop doing)

_____

_____

___ Keep doing actions (Actions you currently do now and should keep doing)

_____

_____

___ Start doing actions (Actions you don't do now but should start doing)

_____

_____

___ Who will do new actions? (Assign the action to yourself or someone else)

_____

_____

___ By when? (When will these actions be complete?)

_____

_____

"As a child, you may have been told that 'money doesn't grow on trees.' But it can. If you have an orange tree, you can sell oranges."
-Mike Agugliaro

WARRIOR POWER

"By lunch on the first day I said "Mike, I don't give a s**t, I am coming into the Warrior Group". I've been searching for this. I attended other things. I have not joined another group. There are some big groups out there that a lot of companies are joining. I kept hearing the same thing from people I know, "I get in, I start doing stuff, the coaches disappear, there's no help".

I'm sincerely grateful to Mike, I owe him like you can't believe, but it's not for everybody. It's only for people that want to take action. It's not something you're going to come in here, and just sit down, and not be a part of it, not contribute, and not want to move forward. That's not really a warrior mentality."

Glenn Dickey Jr.

WHY YOUR SERVICE BUSINESS SUCKS #3: THE WAY YOU WERE TAUGHT TO LEAD IS ALL WRONG

Every day your employees show up and head out to their desks or to customers' homes to do their work. But how do they know what to do?

They're led. By a leader. That leader is you.

The work of a service business owner is to lead the team. Unfortunately, few service business owners focus on developing leadership skills and instead develop a bruise on their forehead for hitting their head against the wall because of their frustrating team.

It's not your fault. Chances are, you started your business or perhaps inherited it because you came up through the ranks as a service tech. You got your qualifications, you worked at customers' homes, and you either started your business or it was passed on to you. The focus, for your entire career, has been on trade excellence. Nowhere in there did you have to learn how to lead a team.

Some people are born with some natural leadership ability but most people need to learn it. Leadership is a learned skill and you can develop your skills to be the leader that your employees want to look to.

If you want to create a smooth-running business that serves customers, then the most important thing you can do as an owner is to step up and lead your team.

What Is A Leader?

I use the word "leader" very intentionally here. I avoid the word "boss" and focus on "leader."

An illustration that works great for a leader is one of those ancient warships where rowers move in unison to propel a ship forward. Rowers are seated backwards on the ship and can't see where they're going. And, they need to move in perfect unison to move the ship forward. If a rower gets out of sync, the oars stop rowing and the ship doesn't move forward. Meanwhile, the leader is the one at the top of ship who can see where the ship is going and he directs the rowers to work together to move the ship.

What a picture of leadership! The rowers are each focused on their own individual tasks, the leader needs to see the whole picture – both the work of the rowing team as well as the direction of the ship – and makes sure each rower does the work required of them.

A leader can't leave the rowers on their own because the rowers will not work in unison and don't know where they're going. And the rowers may not realize it but they rely on the leader to direct them, or else there is chaos below decks.

As the service business owner, you are the leader and your employees are the rowers. You need to keep one eye fixed on the direction of your business and your other eye fixed on how your team is working to make sure they work together.

If you spend each day working on these two important areas of focus, you'll be surprised at what your company achieves.

But now you're wondering, "How do I do that? How do I lead my team?" Here's how…

Inspire Your Team

Some business owners never fully learn the strategies of being a leader so their idea of leadership is very dictatorial: they tell an employee to do something and then they deliver a harsh rebuke if the employee varies at all;

while some don't bother guiding their employees at all and then wonder why nothing gets done.

The best form of leadership is one that inspires your team. Do you live, act, and work in the manner that you want your employees to be? Are you the ideal model that your employees aspire to be like?

I believe that employees rise to the level of the leader they follow. And if there's a characteristic that your employees consistently struggle with, chances are the you may also struggle with that aspect as well. (Perhaps not consciously.)

For example, do you get frustrated by your employees' work ethic? Then answer this question as honestly as possible: what do they see you doing? You might work hard but it might not be evident to your employees (they may not see your work as "work" or you may do it all behind closed doors so they never see you working). Or, if you have concerns about whether your employees interact appropriately with customers – take an honest look at yourself and figure out whether your employees see you interacting with someone and they're modeling their behavior after you.

As a leader, you need to inspire your team. One of the best ways to do this is for you to first create a vision of what the future of your company can be like and then share that vision with your employees. Share it with them right from their very first day working for you and help them see what a career at your company could be like. Get them excited about a shared future and see themselves contributing to make it a reality.

One of the most important things you can do is to invest in yourself and your own education. If your employees see you consistently investing in your own ongoing education to learn to grow the company and be a better leader, you'll model an inspirational example of someone who always strives to be better. Isn't that the kind of employee you want working for you? Inspire them!

I frequently hear back from people who attend my 4-day Warrior Fast Track Academy events and they report that they return from these events with a higher level of inspiration and motivation, which, in turn, inspires their employees to rise to the occasion. I love to hear that!

Leadership 101

Once you've stepped up to inspire your team and you've created an exciting vision of the future for them, then leadership becomes about periodic course corrections to ensure that the whole team is working toward that inspiring future.

The next parts of leadership are surprisingly simple, but take some discipline, patience, and strict scheduling to maintain.

Based on your vision, turn it into clear and measurable targets – annual targets, quarterly targets, monthly targets, daily targets. Make sure everyone's targets contribute to the overall vision.

Share those targets with each person and make them aware of the importance of those targets as well as the fact that they will be measured by them. Create incentives (such as contests) around those targets and get your team excited about achieving them.

Regularly measure your team against those targets and review those measurements with each team member during a quarterly review. This helps to keep your team on track and allows you to identify problems where some employees might be falling behind – you can make sure they have the resources necessary to get back on track.

Of course I'm just scratching the surface of what leadership is but if you're struggling with your team then perhaps it's your leadership that needs to be adjusted. Fortunately, this is a learned skill and many of the components of leadership are covered in my book *Secrets Of Leadership Mastery*.

You'll also discover more leadership strategies and inspiration at the Warrior Fast Track Academy event – which is a great place to develop your skills and see how I lead my team.

Want some help with your leadership? We're currently booking free 30 minute one-on-one strategy calls with a Master Coach Trainer who would be happy to talk to you about how you can lead your team. Schedule your free 30 minute strategy call with a Master Coach Trainer at: www.warriortoday.com

Take Action!

Recommended actions:

__ Look at all the elements that make up your brand. What message does it communicate?

_____

_____

___ What are your competitors' brands like?

_____

_____

___ What could you do differently that would help you stand out?

_____

_____

___ What would a Fortune 500 version of your brand look like?

_____

_____

___ **Schedule your free 30 minute strategy call with a Master Coach Trainer at www.warriortoday.com**

Add your own actions:

___ Stop doing actions (Actions you currently do now but should stop doing)

_____

_____

___ Keep doing actions (Actions you currently do now and should keep doing)

_____

_____

__ Start doing actions (Actions you don't do now but should start doing)

_____

_____

__ Who will do new actions? (Assign the action to yourself or someone else)

_____

_____

__ By when? (When will these actions be complete?)

_____

_____

"Stop trying to be your employees' boss. Stop trying to be their friend. Instead, create an inspiring vision and get your team clear and aligned on that vision. You'll create an unstoppable force in your company that pushes forward with strength. THAT is how to lead."

-Mike Agugliaro

WARRIOR POWER

"Mike has taught me how to cross pollinate in all 3 trades together, opening up my eyes and teaching me how to teach each one of my techs, how to look out for the other trade and drive business and drive the marketing cost down. The results have been phenomenal."

Ted Puzio 2nd Year Warrior

WHY YOUR BUSINESS SUCKS #4: YOU WERE NEVER TAUGHT HOW TO BUILD A STRATEGIC PLAN

Does your business frustrate you sometimes? Perhaps you know something is broken but you're not sure how to fix it, or maybe you are enjoying success at a certain level but can't quite break through to the next level. Maybe you have a vision for the future but you just can translate it into action.

You're not alone. This happens a lot. Service business owners often bump into the obstacle of trying to turn a target, goal, or idea into something that they can actually implement and grow in their business.

Instead of taking a laser-focused approach, most service business owners use the "shotgun method" for everything they do: whether hiring and training, marketing and lead generating, building sales programs and promotions, and refining their customer service, and managing their money… the process is almost always the same: they just do whatever they think of at the time, or the latest technique they heard somewhere.

So, one day you hear that coupons are working well so you create a coupon. Then the next day you hear that free inspections are working well so make a free inspection offer. Then the next day you hear that customers are responding to postcards so you send out postcards. Then the next day you hear that past customers are ordering a certain type of system when it's sold in a certain way so you add that to your offer.

On and on it goes – day after day – until you reach the point you're at now: frustrated and fed up and wondering why it's not working for you the way it works for other people.

I can tell you the reason: it's because the shotgun approach has you firing out one technique after another, without any plan or overall methodology.

The best approach is to create a strategic plan and then implement that plan. Unfortunately, very few service business owners learn to do that. Even the industry organizations and groups fail to educate service business owners on how to build a strategic plan – so it's no surprise that people who attend the Warrior Fast Track Academy frequently tell me that learning to build a strategic plan was one of the big game-changers for them.

So, how do you build a strategic plan?

Vision To Action

Start with a strong, clear vision of what you want to accomplish in your business (and in your life.) Get a crystal clear picture in your mind of what your business will be like in the future – say, 5 years down the road. See it as clearly in your mind as if you were really there.

Next, break down that vision into various components. For example:

- How many people work at your company?
- How many vehicles are in your fleet?
- How much money does your company make?
- How many customers do you have?
- How big is your service area?
- What trade-lines do you offer?
- How do you fit in the picture? (i.e. Do you still show up every day? What hours do you work? Is your family supportive of the company?)

Now that you've broken it down into various components, then take each of those components and reverse-engineer them into yearly, quarterly, monthly, and daily targets.

For example, let's say you plan to make $10 million a year (five years from now), and you currently make $1 million a year. Breaking that down, you might expect to grow from $1 million this year to $3 million in year 2, $5 million in year 3, $7 million in year 4 and $10 million in year 5.

Now look at next year's $2 million target. That's a $250,000 each quarter, or about $83,333 each month, or about $2,777 each day.

With that daily number you can do a lot!

- Figure out how many customers you need to serve daily in order to hit your target.
- Figure out how much marketing you need to do to get those customers.
- Make sure you have enough staff to serve those customers.
- Make sure your staff are equipped to handle the higher volume of work and to effective sell and serve your customers.
- Measure your staff against how much income they need to generate per customer.
- Make sure you have enough vehicles in your fleet to meet that volume of work.
- Make sure your vendors are ready to deliver the products and supplies you need (remember: you're basically doubling your sales over this year.)

Building a strategic plan starts with gaining a clear vision of what you want, turning that vision into specific, measurable components, reverse engineering those components into small, manageable numbers, and then apply those numbers to your business.

Those who attend the Warrior Fast Track Academy get a **90 Day Warrior Road Map, which is a strategic plan for the next 90 days. This Road Map is a powerful, proven tool to help you build a strategic plan and then deploy it effectively.** What Warrior Fast Track attendees love is: it's not a generic plan where I just hand you a list of things to do. Rather, YOU actually build your own Road Map over the course of the 4-day event (I show you how) and there are Master Coach Trainers there who can guide you as well. We even review the Road Map and we won't let you leave until you have it all dialed in and ready to implement – that's how serious my team and I are at making sure you're equipped to grow your business strategically.

Maybe you have some questions about strategy or you want to start building a strategic plan before you even get to the Warrior Fast Track Academy. We're currently booking free 30 minute one-on-one strategy calls with a Master Coach Trainer who would be happy to talk to you about how to build a strategic plan in your business. Schedule your free 30 minute strategy call with a Master Coach Trainer at: www.warriortoday.com

Take Action!

Recommended actions:

__ Develop a strong vision for your company for the next 5 years. Start making notes below (but you'll probably want to make more notes on a larger sheet of paper.)

_____

_____

__ Reverse engineer that vision into smaller components and then into something measurable.

__ **Schedule your free 30 minute strategy call with a Master Coach Trainer at <u>www.warriortoday.com</u>**

Add your own actions:

__ Stop doing actions (Actions you currently do now but should stop doing)

_____

_____

__ Keep doing actions (Actions you currently do now and should keep doing)

_____

_____

__ Start doing actions (Actions you don't do now but should start doing)

_____

_____

__ Who will do new actions? (Assign the action to yourself or someone else)

_____

_____

__ By when? (When will these actions be complete?)

_____

_____

"Most business owners struggle through each day with little more than a vague notion of what they want to achieve. Warriors have a crystal-clear vision for the next 5 years, 1 year, 1 quarter, 1 month, and 1 day… and they execute relentlessly to achieve their vision."

-Mike Agugliaro

Get the latest strategies for free at CEOWARRIOR.com…

WARRIOR POWER

"I came here last November, I'm getting ready to go on my second year. Same thing with a lot of the other guys, I've been with some other groups, and it's been unbelievable the first year. Not only the business stuff that you get, but it's life changing too. My marriage, not that I was getting divorced or anything, but it just brought my marriage to like a level 10 after that, it's like holy cow.

Mike holds you accountable. Like Ted said, how does he have time. He gets back to you ... this isn't like a rah-rah fest, take your money and you're not going to see him. If you need something tomorrow he's there. I know I had an issue with an employee in July. I knew Mike was at the beach but this was a serious issue, I didn't really know how to handle it. I texted Mike and he gets back to me while he's at the beach with his family. This is the commitment we have."

Dustin Folkes 2nd Year Warrior

WHY YOUR BUSINES SUCKS #5:
YOUR COMPETITORS SEEM TO BE HIRING ALL THE GOOD PEOPLE

I hear this all the time from service business owners, "it's so hard to find great employees… only my competitors with the deepest pockets can afford to pay them."

Have you ever thought that? Have you ever wondered if you were giving up good employees because you couldn't afford to pay them enough?

Here's something that might surprise you: most service business owners get pretty focused on how much they can or can't afford to pay, and when the get frustrated with their existing employees they find that their pay levels become an easy thing to blame and they assume that a higher pay would finally mean getting the top performers they really want.

But nothing could be further from the truth. In fact, your payroll budget is actually just an excuse (even though you might not realize it). **You'll be surprised to discover that pay is only one small part of the reasons that someone chooses to work for you or not work for you.**

Yes, even the top performers.

There are many reasons why people work for you even if you can't pay top dollar.

For example:

- A smaller service area might be preferable to some because that means they have less traveling to do.
- Some companies require their staff to sell really hard, using aggressive sales tactics. If you don't have that selling approach, your employees might prefer that.
- Flexible shifts can be attractive to some people, particularly if they have other commitments outside of work – such as family responsibilities.
- Perhaps you can't offer top-grade pay but you do offer amazing benefits. Some employees will accept a lower level of pay because of the benefits that are available at your company, which could save them money.
- Another benefit you can offer is better training – your employees will love getting educated and honing their skills, which will make them more competitive in the job market and more valuable to you as the employer.
- Some employees don't want to just be a cog in a big machine but prefer the family atmosphere of a smaller company, where they can be on a first-name-basis with the owner.
- A strong culture where everyone works together (and even hangs out after work together) can also be a compelling draw for some employees.

Those are just some strategies that you can use. There are many more. And I'll also share two of my very best strategies that you should definitely be using if you're a smaller company or one that doesn't pay as much as your competitors:

- **Faster career growth** – in smaller companies top performers can rise faster, so make sure you have a great career path laid out for you're A-Players to aspire to!
- **Recognition** – make sure you frequently and publicly recognize members of your team. Heck, even put their name and picture in the newspaper every time they have a major success or promotion.

Hiring an amazing team is not about how much you can pay them. Yes, paying them well can be beneficial but remember that many of your prospective employees do not all place the same value on a high paycheck that you think they do. There are many reasons why they work for you.

If you want to know how to attract more employees to your company without boosting your payroll, simply ask your current top performers why they work for you. Get them to list as many reasons as possible and see how you can work those into your hiring efforts.

Want to get some additional strategies about how to hire A-players and build a high-performing team? Schedule your free 30 minute one-on-one strategy call with a Master Coach Trainer at: www.warriortoday.com

Take Action!

Recommended actions:

__ What is better about you than your competitors?

_____

_____

__ What are the frustrations you face in your company around hiring A players?

_____

_____

__ Schedule your free 30 minute strategy call with a Master Coach Trainer at www.warriortoday.com

Add your own actions:

___ Stop doing actions (Actions you currently do now but should stop doing)

_____

_____

___ Keep doing actions (Actions you currently do now and should keep doing)

_____

_____

___ Start doing actions (Actions you don't do now but should start doing)

_____

_____

___ Who will do new actions? (Assign the action to yourself or someone else)

_____

_____

___ By when? (When will these actions be complete?)

_____

_____

WARRIOR POWER

"It was instant for me, it just hit because I felt like Mike wasn't here to sell me anything, he was here to help me. He opened his arms up, opened everything up. It's a brotherhood here. It's not a group, it's not an association. It's a brotherhood. When you join the Warrior group, it's a brotherhood.

It's been a lot of struggles up and down and you just kind of go with the flow. Because of this, I've been able to make a lot of changes. There's a lot of changes that have happened internally, but the biggest change that has happened is with me personally."

Jamie Miller 2nd Year Warrior

WHY YOUR SERVICE BUSINESS SUCKS #6: WHY YOUR RECRUITING AND HIRING SUCKS

Does it ever feel like a struggle to find the right people? Maybe you're not sure if they're out there, or maybe you wonder if you'll find someone who is as dedicated as you.

Sure, you might have a couple of good employees, but there probably seems to be more frustrating ones. And chances are, you're stuck between a rock and a hard place: you could get rid of the frustrating ones but then you won't have enough people to serve your customers; or, you could keep the frustrating employees but you know that they're just not delivering the best service.

And chances are, you already know that it starts with your recruiting and hiring practices. How do you hire the best employees when you only have so many people to draw from. Are the good employees all taken?

You'll be glad to know that there are good employees out there – really hardworking employees who step up and deliver as much or more than you were expecting… and you'll also be glad to know that you can hire these people without having to pay them a fortune.

So, how do you find, recruit, and hire the employees you want to hire while at the same time passing over the ones you don't want to hire. How do you find the cream of the crop and add them to your team? How do you recruit and hire "A players" to work for you?

Well, before I give you some specific strategies, let me point out one often-overlooked step: do you REALLY want A-players? Many service business owners think they want the best employees but then they're shocked by A-players who turn out to be natural leaders and independent thinkers who are confident and able to work on their own. That's the true A-player – they're trainable, yes, but they're also highly independent hard workers. You might discover, like many service business owners, that you say you want A-players but you really want a "worker bee" who just follows your commands to the letter. So before you keep reading in this chapter, make sure you think carefully about who you really want to work for you. Personally, **I want A-players and I know that I'll have to sometimes corral them because they're strong and forceful leaders and independent thinkers – I love that**! But you need to be prepared to be the right leader for these people. (I talk about various leadership strategies in my book *Secrets Of Leadership Mastery*) to help service business owners become stronger leaders for their team.

Identify Your A-Players

You probably wish for great employees but have you actually defined what a great employee looks like? In marketing, we create a picture of the ideal customer (we call it an "avatar") – you need to do the same thing in your recruiting. Figure out who your ideal employee is.

- What are they like?
- What do they look like? (Young? Do they have facial hair?)
- What do they sound like? (Educated? Friendly?)
- What do they know?
- What don't they know?
- What certifications and qualifications do they have?
- What level of experience do they have?
- When are they available to work?
- What do they like to do in their spare time?

There are some of the questions you should be asking to identify your ideal employee. If you're not sure of the answers to these questions, think about who your best employees are right now (or the good ones you've had in the past) and figure out what was similar about all of them.

For example, you might decide that the best employees are right out of school and very hungry to make their mark in the industry but have no bad habits learned from a previous employer; or, you might decide that the best employee has previous military experience and is now looking to start a career; or you might decide that your employees are older and more experienced with a passion for hunting and fishing.

All of this information is helpful because some of it might help you determine where to find these people (such as a Veterans Affairs office if you're looking for people with military experience) or it might help you determine how to make the job offer more attractive to the prospective employee (such as time off during hunting season if you're looking for hunters).

At my 4-day Warrior Fast Track Academy we talk about the best employees and I walk attendees through the steps to create an employee avatar and how to recruit these people.

Be The Company They Want To Work For

When coaching service business owners, I often hear their frustration that they can't find good employees to work for them. They're confident that as soon as the good employees show up, their business will finally run the way they want it to.

This is not true, however. **You don't add good employees and THEN get a great business. It's the other way around: you create a strong business and good employees get added to it.** (If you were at my Warrior Fast Track Academy, you'd hear a roomful of business owners shout "Boom!" to the massive mind-shift I just shared.)

Before you even start searching for your perfect employee, take a long, hard look at your business and **ask yourself whether it's the company that good employees want to work at.**

Consider it from the employee's perspective: let's say you're an up-and-coming A-player who is willing to work hard. You don't mind putting in the hours and even accepting slightly lower pay at first if it means a longer-term opportunity with a great company. So, you send out your resume for a job and you get two companies:

- One company has amazing employees you can learn from, a great reputation you can be proud of, and plenty of opportunities in the future. You also know that they measure their employees quarterly against milestones to ensure that everyone is doing their best – and you love the idea that your hard work will be recognized and rewarded.

- The other company has so-so employees that you may end up training (that's okay but you also want to learn, too), a less-than-amazing reputation, and you're not sure how long you'll work there. Plus, there are no clear quarterly measurements, which suggests to you that family members or friends who work there might have a better chance at being promoted than someone with the skills and work ethic that you bring to the table.

As an A-player, which company do you think is more attractive and more likely that you'd prefer to work for?

Now as the owner of a service business, which of these two companies is your service business more like? Sure, I've described two extremes on a spectrum, but which company is yours closer to? Chances are, if you're not hiring the employees you want to be hiring, your company isn't the company that is structured to attract A-players.

Start with your perfect employee avatar and think about what you want in a great employee. Then think about what that employee will want in an employer. Now build your company in a way is the business your best employees want to work for.

Hold A Recruiting Event

One powerful way to hire great people is to hold a recruiting event. This is a powerful, strategic way to find only the best employees and I use it regularly to hire A-players. (Service business owners who have seen me run these in the past always say that it changes the hiring game for them.)

Here's how it works: Once you've collected a bunch of resumes, invite them in for an interview. But here's the thing – don't invite them in for separate interviews, *invite them all in for the same interview!*

Hold an event at your office or even in a local rented conference room, and bring in a dozen or more applicants. Introduce yourself and give them an overview of what your company is like. Then talk to the audience and ask them questions.

This event is very powerful because **you find out very quickly who the natural leaders are and who brings a level of confidence to this unusual situation.** (Hint: that's probably the A-player that you want to hire.) At the same time, people who are scared off from this unusual situation will stay quiet, hold back, and may even take their own name out of the running because they realize it's not for them.

Recruiting and hiring is a mystery for many service business owners because they don't always know who they want to work for them or how to find those people. I've just scratched the surface of several strategies I use to find A-players for my service business, I've talked about some of these strategies on MSNBC, and I teach these same strategies at my 4-day Warrior Fast Track Academy event

Want some help with your recruiting and hiring? We're currently booking free 30 minute one-on-one strategy calls with a Master Coach Trainer who would be happy to talk to you about how to create a stronger recruiting program to finally hire A-players. Schedule your free 30 minute strategy call with a Master Coach Trainer at: www.warriortoday.com

Take Action!

Recommended actions:

__ What does an A-player look like for your company?

_____

_____

__ Plan a recruiting event to find new people for your company.

__ Schedule your free 30 minute strategy call with a Master Coach Trainer at www.warriortoday.com

Add your own actions:

__ Stop doing actions (Actions you currently do now but should stop doing)

_____

_____

__ Keep doing actions (Actions you currently do now and should keep doing)

_____

_____

__ Start doing actions (Actions you don't do now but should start doing)

_____

_____

__ Who will do new actions? (Assign the action to yourself or someone else)

_____

_____

__ By when? (When will these actions be complete?)

_____

_____

"Do you really want A-players in your company? You may think you do… but many business owners really want someone who follows directions and does what they're told. A-players are a breed of leaders and you need to be prepared to lead these top performers – it's a completely different type of employee than you're probably used to leading."

-Mike Agugliaro

WARRIOR POWER

"Rarely do you get the kind of value and commitment that is apparent in what Mike provides and the impact it's had on our company.

Thank you for making a difference in our company, the lives of our staff, (who are becoming better versions of themselves) and finally our clients who are getting world class service."

Andy Rodenhiser

WHY YOUR BUSINESS SUCKS #7: YOUR TEAM IS NOT PRODUCTIVE AND THEY JUST END UP DOING THEIR OWN THING

When you first started your service business, you might have had an optimistic idea about what your employees would be like and how they'd perform at work.

Did you discover a different experience once you'd started hiring people? Many service business owners do. Simply put: Many employees show up (sometimes late), they don't seem as motivated as they did when they were being interviewed for the job, they often do their own thing or disregard what you ask them to do, and they leave early.

Ironically, if you put in as little effort into getting their paychecks to them as they did earning their paychecks, you'd have a revolt!

Sure, not all of them are like this but many are. Unfortunately you're stuck between a rock and hard place because you can't just fire all of your employees and try to replace them – firing everyone would leave you without any workers and replacing them would just mean more of the same problems.

I felt exactly this frustration in my service business years ago – and I only had an assistant! Today my company has over 190 staff and we're always hiring. Not only that but our staff are fiercely loyal and very hard workers. So what's the difference?

It starts with a simple question: "Why?"

Know Their Why

Why do your employees show up to work?

You might say it's because they want to receive a paycheck, but that's not entirely correct. **Your employees don't need the money. They need something that money buys.** What is it? When you find out, you've discovered their true reason for working with you.

Maybe they have a growing family so they work to earn a paycheck to put food on the table and pay the mortgage. Or maybe they're putting a kid through college. Or maybe they're taking care of an ailing parent. Or maybe they have a hobby that they spend their money and time on.

Whatever they spend their money on, and whatever they spend their time doing when they aren't working – that's their "**why**" for showing up to work.

Unfortunately for most people, they experience a disconnect between their "why" and their work. They forget that their paycheck gives them the money and free time to do the things that are important to them.

As a leader, one of the most effective things you can do is figure out each employee's "why" and then help them see the connection between their work and their why.

When you discover the "why" of each of your team members, you can inspire them to give their very best to you so you can help them enjoy or fulfill their "why."

This "why" discovery and this idea of serving will change everything: it helps you find and recruit the best team members, it helps you motivate and inspire your team, and it will even help you let someone go from your company.

When you're recruiting, you can determine your prospective new-hire's "why" and then point out how you'll help them achieve it. (That will put you head-and-shoulders above any other company they're thinking about working for).

When you're motivating and inspiring your team, you can point out how their hard work enables you to pay them and give them job security, which can help them to enjoy their "why".

And, if an employee is not performing at the level they need to be, you can take a different approach than getting angry and firing them – instead, you can ask them about their "why" and how their work has helped to support it. Some employees might see the connection and step up again; and if any employees doesn't see the connection and change their ways, you can relocate them out of your company and suggest they find a company where the work can help to support their "why".

I love this approach to running a business. When you step up as a leader, you build a team who gives their very best because they achieve their own goals. And when your team gives their very best, your customers are served. And when your customers are served, your business grows. Everyone wins.

If you want to create a service business that you dreamed of owning – where every employee acts in an aligned manner to represent your business to your customers, the best way to get everyone moving in the same direction is to know their "why".

I've only scratched the surface about leadership, culture, and team-building but I know what I'm saying resonates with people because I spoke about it on MSNBC and people loved it. There's so much more (although I've shared a great place to start). If you'd like to talk about how to get your team moving in the same direction in your business then schedule a complimentary strategy call with a Master Coach Trainer at: www.warriortoday.com

Take Action!

Recommended actions:

__ What are the frustrations you face in your recruiting and hiring?

_____

_____

__ What do you wish your team could be like?

_____

_____

__ Schedule your free 30 minute strategy call with a Master Coach Trainer at www.warriortoday.com

Add your own actions:

__ Stop doing actions (Actions you currently do now but should stop doing)

_____

_____

__ Keep doing actions (Actions you currently do now and should keep doing)

_____

_____

__ Start doing actions (Actions you don't do now but should start doing)

_____

_____

__ Who will do new actions? (Assign the action to yourself or someone else)

_____

_____

__ By when? (When will these actions be complete?)

_____

_____

WARRIOR POWER

"When Mike coached me, it was all the right stuff at the right time. Mike has no problem saying, 'stop being an idiot' when he's coaching me, and he'll kick me in the ass when I need to be reeled back in. When I get too far ahead of myself and want to do step seven, he'll remind me that I need to do steps one through six first."

Steven Addario

WHY YOUR BUSINESS SUCKS #8: YOUR CUSTOMERS HAVE NO LOYALTY – THEY JUST CALL THE FIRST COMPANY THEY THINK OF… AND IT'S NOT ALWAYS YOU

Customer loyalty has shifted. It's not what it once was. Decades ago, there were only a few businesses in a single area and people knew each other on a first name basis.

Today, there's so much more choice and complexity, and people are exposed to so much more marketing than they ever were before.

And, there's something else that's shifted too: many service businesses claim to be more focused than ever on customer service yet what they consider to be consider service has fallen far short of what it should be.

I always say that **service is one degree worse than you think it is** – so if you're trying to provide "good customer service" to your customers, you're only providing mediocre customer service at best.

Many service businesses pride themselves on good customer service like knowing the customer's name or always being polite. If that's what you're striving for, here's the shocking news: **you might think you're doing something amazing but you're not. You're doing the barest minimum that 99% of all other service businesses are doing. As a result your customers can't tell your business apart from all the others.**

The cost is tremendous: you end up marketing over and over to get one customer in the door, and then you have to spend all that money again to get the next customer in the door. This is a huge waste of marketing dollars and effort. If you could only create enough **loyalty** so that your customers would remember you and even refer you to their friends and family, you'd save money on marketing and you'd make more money per customers.

So what can you do? The truth is: **you need to SHOCK your customers with service that is so stunning and outrageously remarkable that they are left nearly speechless when you leave, and they run to their phone to call all their friends to say, "you won't believe the service I just received!"**

Think about all the ways you can serve your customers, now do 1000% more. At some point you'll think, "*oh, that's too much*" and when you get to that point, **you'll be getting close to the level of service that will actually generate loyalty.**

One of the most powerful ways to create loyalty is to build what I call a **"Framework For WOW Service"**. This framework outlines the steps you take to serve your customer. It starts with the marketing you do and continues through every aspect of the interaction to the point when you are calling them back to offer them additional services in the future.

The keys to a good Framework For Service is: it needs to be detailed (mine even goes minute-by-minute when my expert arrives at the customer's house), and it needs to have WOW service baked right in.

By doing this, I make sure that I control the customer interaction and I leave nothing to chance or to what my employee feels like doing that day; it also ensures that I'm focused on serving my customer always; and it creates a consistent experience for every customer.

Below, I've shared part of my company's Framework For WOW Service (along with some helpful explanations) but this is just a small selection – the real one is many pages long.

Framework For WOW Service

Pre-rapport Formula: about 15 to 20 minutes before the scheduled visit, my expert will call the customer and say, "I'll be there in about 15 to 20 minutes. I understand you're having problem with your water heater, tell me about it." And they'll listen to the customer. And then they'll offer something friendly like, "Hey, I'm passing a coffee shop, can I get you a coffee?"

This step prepares the customer, and the expert, and it builds additional rapport with a friendly offer of coffee.

Say Hello: when my expert arrives at the prospective customer's house, they greet the customer. "Hi, I'm Mike from Gold Medal Service. Nice to meet you. Is it okay where my vehicle is parked? Do you have any dogs or cats I should be aware of? Do you have any time restraints that might impact how much time we have to work? Is there anyone else that should be involved in this?"

This step is friendly and very service-oriented. And, it tells the expert a lot: like if the person had a time restraint, perhaps the expert needs to move a little more quickly through the visit. Or if someone else should be involved in the process, perhaps the expert needs to arrange a different time to visit so that the spouse (for example) is also at home.

Discovery: during this step, the expert learns all they can about the situation. They're asking questions – not just about the specific problem but about the larger picture. (You'll see in a moment why this is important). For example, the expert might ask, "How old is the water heater?" And, "Has it given you any problems in the past?" And, "Has anyone worked on it before?" And, "Does it give you enough water?"

These questions are key because anyone can go in and fix the immediate problem but by asking more questions about the broader situation, the expert might be able to recommend a completely different solution – one that fits the customer even better. In this example, perhaps the hot water heater is broken and the prospective customer called for a repair. But by asking questions, the expert might discover that it never really gave enough hot water for the entire family anyway. Remember, we're not trying to solve a one-time problem for a one-time customer. We're building a relationship because we want to serve this customer for their lifetime. This is a very different approach and it helps us to provide solutions that are of a higher, longer-lasting value to the customer (and to our business).

The answers to the questions in the discovery step will help in the recommendation, next...

Recommendation: in this step, the expert makes a few recommendations based on the best solutions for the prospective customer's problems.

- First, the expert would say: "Let me tell you about myself and the company" and then briefly talk about how the company helps other customers.
- Then the expert would say, "Let me tell you what I heard you say," and they'd repeat back what the customer said. This kind of confirmation is helpful to ensure that the

expert has correctly heard the customer's concerns, and it gives the customer another opportunity to add any other problems they are facing.

- Then the expert would say: "Here are a few options. Let's see what fits for you and your family." And with that, the expert lays out a few options that they believe the customer would benefit from.
- And last, the expert asks the customer which solution they would prefer.

The customer will choose something that they are comfortable with, that fits their budget, and that solves their problem. This is not some sales technique. This is a serving-first communication tool and system to help people think through the process of what they should consider.

While other businesses might call this a "closing technique" as part of a sales pitch, we think of this very differently: We're always serving and this recommendation comes from a service mindset. We don't have to sell or close the customer because the WOW service we provide closes itself.

Get it done: now it's time to get the job done. This is important because the customer is watching to see what the expert is doing! Are they doing what they promised? Are they respectful of the customer's house? Are they communicating what they are doing? That's what the customer is watching for, so the expert will use a tarp, keep the area clean, keep the customer informed of what they are doing and what the timeline is like. And when the expert is done, they'll clean up and vacuum the area. The expert's service and attentiveness and ability to solve the problem will confirm for the customer that the customer made a great decision.

Finish it up: in this step, the expert will explain what they did and how they did it, and then they'll talk about the existing things the company also does for its customers. Then the expert will talk about referrals – how referrals from the customer are appreciated and encouraged. Finally, the expert will make sure the customer is happy with the work and they'll complete the payment and close out the job.

Neighborhood Impact: the expert will complete some simple marketing activities in the neighborhood. For example, the expert will put out door hangers, yard signs, and even say hello to the neighbors.

This Framework For WOW Service is a powerful tool and I recommend that you build something like it into your business. (You don't have to build it exactly the same, as long as you have good reasons for building the steps that you do choose to build.)

As you think about delivering WOW service to your customer, you may ask yourself a question that many service business owners ask at this point: when am I spending too much money or time with each customer? Doesn't that make each job less profitable?

If you're wondering that, here's my answer: **You're still thinking of customers as transactional one-time-only customers. That makes each customer very expensive. I, on the other hand, think of my customers as lifetime customers who I will market to once, until they're in the door, then I'll serve them with generous WOW service and they'll buy from me over and over and send their friends and family to me. This drives down the cost to acquire each customer, and makes each customer far more profitable to serve.**

When you're focused on it, it's so simple and straightforward to provide amazing service to your customers. Besides, the way you've been doing until now may be working AGAINST you instead of FOR you! So revisit your service and create WOW service.

If you want to talk about how to improve the serve you deliver to your customers, you can schedule a free 30 minute strategy call with a Master Coach Trainer at: www.warriortoday.com

Take Action!

Recommended actions:

__ Create a Framework For WOW Service.

__ What are the frustrations you face with your customers' loyalty?

_____

_____

__ Schedule your free 30 minute strategy call with a Master Coach Trainer at www.warriortoday.com

Add your own actions:

___ Stop doing actions (Actions you currently do now but should stop doing)

_____

_____

___ Keep doing actions (Actions you currently do now and should keep doing)

_____

_____

___ Start doing actions (Actions you don't do now but should start doing)

_____

_____

___ Who will do new actions? (Assign the action to yourself or someone else)

_____

_____

___ By when? (When will these actions be complete?)

_____

_____

"Most business owners think that shockingly good service is 'too much.' I say, that's only the beginning."

-Mike Agugliaro

WARRIOR POWER

"He taught us how to make the phone ring. Run the leads and sell. I probably would still be stuck in a truck by myself. Or, even worse just giving up. Because, I was at that point already. I'm saying, "okay, I'm killing myself here. I'm not getting nowhere". Now, I am getting somewhere. I see a light at the end of the tunnel. After working with Mike our phone rings every day."

Joe Collins 2nd Year Warrior

WHY YOUR BUSINESS SUCKS #9: YOUR BRAND IS WEAK

You fight every single day to capture the attention of customers, convince them to buy from you instead of anyone else, and then hope that they remember your business next time they need your services.

Many service businesses use a combination of marketing to find the customers and customer service to keep them… all while giving little or no thought to their company's brand.

Yet, service businesses that recognize the importance of a brand, soon discover its power: **by investing a bit of time and effort into creating a powerful and memorable brand, you'll more easily attract customers, you'll more easily convince them to buy from your company, and you'll stick in their minds for years to come… And you'll do it all at a lower marketing cost.**

A good brand is very powerful but it's often overlooked by service business owners. In fact, a brand is often misunderstood.

Every company has a brand. No, it's not just the logo, it's so much more. It's the name, the logo, the slogan, and the general emotion or concept that is communicated through these things. It's your company's identity and it needs to communicate to your customers exactly what kind of business you do and what kind of customers you serve.

In fact, not only does a good brand need to identify and communicate to your customers – a good brand is a magnet to the exact customers you want, attracting the best customers to you.

Very few service business owners put much thought into their brand, yet they don't realize how much their existing brand (or lack of it) is potentially hurting them.

Weak brands hurt your business. Think of your customer for a moment: When they need to hire you for service, what do they do? They look in the Yellow Pages or online and they see your brand against several other brands. What does your brand do?

In most cases, your brand just says what you do, and that's it... more importantly, your brand doesn't establish a difference between you and all of your competitors.

As a result, your customer can't tell the difference between you and your competitors so they just call the first company they see, or the one with the biggest ad, or the one with the easiest-to-remember phone number.

Not only that but your brand also tells your customer something about you. An ugly brand repulses customers. A low-end brand attracts low-end customers. A local brand attracts local customers.

... On the other hand, **a beautiful, high-end brand attracts high-end customers, and a brand that isn't tied to a local area can grow bigger.**

So what should you do?

Let me give you a mental picture to help you know exactly what to do about your brand: Imagine you're in a giant stadium and the playing field is covered in yellow balls. If I ask you to find one specific yellow ball, you'll go crazy searching one yellow ball after another. You may never find the specific yellow ball I'm talking about.

But what if, in that sea of yellow balls, there was one black ball and I told you to find that black ball. Would you find it? No problem. You could do it almost instantly, from a distance, without a moment's hesitation.

Likewise, in your market today, **all the home service businesses are a sea of yellow balls. They're almost impossible to tell one from another. And a classic mistake that every service business owner does is to make their service business brand like another yellow ball... maybe because they want to fit in or they don't want to make waves or they don't know any better.**

When I help service business owners to rebrand, I help them build a brand that's the equivalent of a black ball.

... And guess which brand the customers start to notice? Yes, the one that stands out.

When I rebranded Gold Medal Service, my partner and I were trying to figure out what colors to choose. I looked around the market and noticed that no other home service business was using yellow trucks, so we created a logo that was primarily yellow and we painted all our trucks yellow. We stood out.

If your business is struggling to find good customers and to keep them, you might be a yellow ball in a sea of yellow balls. It's time to make a change to your brand and level up the quality and message of your brand.

When you do, you'll discover:

- You'll start getting more leads because you'll stand out
- You'll start attracting more of the right customers
- Your customers will remember you
- Even your marketing costs could decline or be spent elsewhere because more and more people recognize your trucks and uniforms and billboards and direct mail

Note: from time to time you may need to do a brand refresh. That's because, over time, your customers and potential customers might become blind to your brand, or some of your brand elements might become outdated or stale, or because your competitors have raised their branding and now many of you are the same colored ball again. Schedule time to look at your brand occasionally and work with a service business branding expert to help you take your brand to the next level.

Here's A Strategy To Take Your Brand To The Next Level

If you want to grow your service business, one of first things you should do is build a brand that supports your growth trajectory.

Think about what vision you have for your company, which I had you write out earlier in this book. Now **think about whether the brand you have now is really the brand that can help you achieve that vision.**

Many service business owners have a very simplistic, almost cartoon-like brand, or a logo that was drawn by an amateur. And if you plan to grow your business statewide or even nationally, will your brand fit in?

Think about companies like Apple, Netflix, FedEx, McDonald's, and General Motors. What do those company's brands look like?

Or google "Google logo history" and check out the transformation of Google's logo over the years. They started out with an amateur logo and transformed it into the current professionally designed (but still fun) logo today.

If you want to grow your business, think about what your brand would look like if it were a Fortune 500 brand. How would it be different?

Want some help with your brand? We're currently booking free 30 minute one-on-one strategy calls with a Master Coach Trainer who

would be happy to talk to you about how you might take your brand to the next level so you can grow your service business with a stronger brand. Schedule your free 30 minute strategy call with a Master Coach Trainer at: www.warriortoday.com

Take Action!

Recommended actions:

___ Look at all the elements that make up your brand. What message does it communicate?

_____

_____

___ What are your competitors' brands like?

_____

_____

___ What could you do differently that would help you stand out?

_____

_____

___ What would a Fortune 500 version of your brand look like?

_____

_____

___ **Schedule your free 30 minute strategy call with a Master Coach Trainer at www.warriortoday.com**

Add your own actions:

__ Stop doing actions (Actions you currently do now but should stop doing)

__ Keep doing actions (Actions you currently do now and should keep doing)

__ Start doing actions (Actions you don't do now but should start doing)

__ Who will do new actions? (Assign the action to yourself or someone else)

__ By when? (When will these actions be complete?)

WARRIOR POWER

"I'm a one-man shop. I've been in business six months. I want to grow quick. I know that I can grow, but I want to grow quick, and I want to do it right. I want to do it with the least amount of headaches possible. The best way to do that is to mimic somebody else. Mike has done that very quickly. I know there was lots of coaches that have grown multi-million dollar businesses, but Mike did it very quickly, in ten years. I'm learning a lot. A lot of things I didn't think I needed to learn. Mainly leadership things. I'm learning that that is the most important, or one of the most important things, to really grow the business.

If you've got a ten million dollar company, you could blow it up into a hundred million dollar company. With these strategies that Mike has, there's no limit."

Mitch Kenney

WHY YOUR BUSINESS SUCKS #10: YOUR MARKETING ISN'T DELIVERING THE LEADS YOU NEED

A lack of customers usually starts because you have a lack of leads. If you can get leads, you can get in front of them and make an offer and some will buy. But if you don't have the leads to begin with (or worse, if you get bad leads), you'll struggle and your service business may eventually die.

The job of your marketing is to generate leads. Unfortunately, service business owners don't do this effectively for one of the following reasons:

- Their marketing is not seen often enough
- Their marketing is not seen by the right people
- Their marketing does not communicate the right message

We'll look at each one of these briefly. I suggest you read through each one and compare it to your current marketing strategies to see how they might be modified.

Your Marketing Is Not Seen Often Enough

This is a huge and costly mistake that service business owners make: they think they need to have their marketing seen by as many people as possible. So, they figure out how much they can afford and they spend that money to spread their marketing across as wide of an area as possible.

Will people respond to that marketing? They might… Or they might not.

Even if the marketing is excellent to begin with, the underlying problem is: It's not how far you spread your marketing, it's how often people see it. Your prospective customers need to see your marketing messages more than once in order for it to have an impact. In fact, they may need to see your marketing a dozen times or more.

If you spend a lot of money to get widespread "reach", your prospective customer may only see your brand once or twice. That's how most service business owners do it.

But I coach people to do it differently. If you spend the exact same amount of money but focus your marketing on a much smaller area in order to get your brand more often in front of the same people, you'll get more leads for the same budget.

As I always say to the service business owners I coach, "**you need to go deep before you go wide**," meaning: you need to market repeatedly to a small set of prospective customers before you start marketing to many prospective customers.

In fact, you can even start marketing over and over and over and over again to just one street or neighborhood. Although this might seem like a waste of money to the uninitiated, you'll discover that it's actually more powerful and effective.

First, people will respond to the frequency and many will eventually buy. (That's because good marketing is a frequency game; frequency builds awareness and trust.)

Second, because you're so focused, you can actually do more service calls in the same day because you're not driving as far.

Third, when a couple of your trucks are parked on the same street every single day, other neighbors will be even further exposed to your brand and will be more likely to call.

Of course you can always grow after that but if your marketing budget is tight yet you want as many good leads as possible, start by focusing your marketing efforts on multiple, frequent marketing to one small area.

Your Marketing Is Not Seen By The Right People

It's tempting to market your service business to anyone and everyone. After all, why would you want to reduce the number of people who can respond to your message?

However, not everyone is the perfect audience for you. If you try to market to everyone, a couple things could happen:

- You'll get some great customers
- You'll also get some less-than-great customers
- You may not get as many customers as you want, because if you try to communicate with everyone, your message will be bland and will not resonate with anyone. (In other words, you can't be all things to all people, as the saying goes.)

If you focus your marketing on your best customers, you can help to filter out the customers you don't want to work with and your marketing becomes clearer and more memorable to those best customers and encourage them to respond.

Think about who your perfect customer is (the one you prefer to work with), and think about who your less-than-perfect customer is (the one you prefer not to work with). The difference between these two people will help you understand how to communicate to your preferred customer.

When thinking about your preferred customer, consider qualities like size and value of home, employment and income, education, and marital and family status. For example, you may want to market to a college educated professional earning $100,000+ per year, who is married with 2 children.

The marketing you do this very specific group will be more specific – and thus more effective – than if you tried to market to anyone and everyone.

This process of thinking about who your best customer is, is called "identifying an avatar." If you talk to a Master Coach Trainer on a strategy call, or if you attend my Warrior Fast Track Academy, you'll hear us talk about avatars and we'll help you identify the best avatars in your business.

In my book, *The Secrets Of Business Mastery*, I describe a few of your avatar's qualities and attributes that you need to identify, including: what they look like, how old are they, where they live, what kind of home they live in, whether they have kids, what kind of car they drive, what kind of job they have, etc.

I gave a good list in that book but you should go as deep as possible and get as much information as you can about this group. The more you know about them, the better you can market to them and the better you can serve them.

Your avatar will shape so much of your business! It will influence the lines of business you have, the people you hire, the prices you charge, the packages/promotions you offer, and even potentially the name of your business.

For example:

- If your perfect customers are first time homeowners who are also new parents, you might market to them about the importance of maintaining a healthy home for their baby; you might call your home inspection package a "busy parent, safe baby" package; you might even ask them on the phone, "when's the baby's nap time so we can make sure we're out of your house before then?"
- If your perfect customers are seniors living in older homes, you might market to them about how challenging and expensive it can be to maintain an efficient and affordable house, and talk about how it takes qualified experts so they don't have to go crawling around their HVAC system to keep it running; you might call your HVAC inspection package a "peace of mind package"; you might market to them and talk about how it's better to spend time with their grandkids than worrying about their house.

If you focus your marketing and know who your avatar is, you're still only part of the way there. You also need to make sure you say the right things.

Your Marketing Does Not Communicate The Right Message

The third problem many service business owners face is: their marketing does not communicate the right message.

The whole purpose of marketing is to get prospective customers calling you to schedule a service call by one of your experts. Make that the primary focus of all your marketing. Avoid the temptation to create marketing that just feels good but doesn't give the prospective customer a reason to call right now.

Your marketing should give them a compelling reason and (ideally) a timeline to create some urgency to get them to call.

Two ways that you can create great marketing that communicates a powerful message include:

- **Education** – educate your prospects and customers with valuable information that helps them make a good decision for the safety and comfort of their family
- **Core Story Marketing** – share the story of why you're in business and how you do business, which will help prospects and customers trust you and feel like they are part of your story.

We talk about both of these things at my 4-day Warrior Fast Track Academy and in the CEO Warrior Circle mastermind group.

If you'd like to talk about how to get more leads in your business then schedule a complimentary strategy call with a Master Coach Trainer at: www.warriortoday.com

Take Action!

Recommended actions:

___ How many times do your prospective customers encounter your brand in a given week?

_____

_____

___ Plan a multi-week sequence of laser-focused marketing.

___ Schedule your free 30 minute strategy call with a Master Coach Trainer at www.warriortoday.com

Add your own actions:

___ Stop doing actions (Actions you currently do now but should stop doing)

_____

_____

__ Keep doing actions (Actions you currently do now and should keep doing)

_____

_____

__ Start doing actions (Actions you don't do now but should start doing)

_____

_____

__ Who will do new actions? (Assign the action to yourself or someone else)

_____

_____

__ By when? (When will these actions be complete?)

_____

_____

"Most business owners think a wide 'net' of marketing will catch the most leads. But my $30+ million a year business proves that laser-focused repetition is far more effective."

-Mike Agugliaro

BONUS CHAPTER:
MAYBE YOU <u>WANT</u> YOUR BUSINESS TO SUCK???

Okay, I'm going to piss some people off with a chapter title like that. They'll say, "Mike, you're crazy – of course I don't want my service business to suck."

Of course I don't mean that you wake up every day dreaming of ways to create more struggle in your business. However, I've found after years of helping to transform many service businesses from struggling into multi-million dollar profit machines, I've learned that many service business owners unintentionally allow their service businesses to suck.

Here's what I mean…

Is Your Goal-Setting Broken?

Perhaps you have an idea of what you want your service business to be like… but how important is that vision to you? Many people set what they believe are goals, resolutions, or have a vision of what they want their service business to do or be. Yet very few turn those goals, resolutions, or visions into reality.

That's why you'll never hear me talk about goal setting, and you'll never hear me make a New Year Resolution. I set targets. **Targets are bullseyes that you focus on and aim to hit.**

So, instead of setting goals, set very specific targets. Set crystal-clear targets that are measurable and actionable. Then revisit them regularly to monitor your progress and course-correct as necessary.

Do You Even Care About Your Targets?

When you set your goals, how important were they to you? Perhaps another way to ask is: how often did you get derailed from them?

Goals are not always very concrete and specific so it's easy to get derailed from them. Targets are more specific so it's easier to focus on them and hit them… But admittedly, it's not automatic. You still need to work at it and you're still at risk of getting pulled off track by the urgent daily problems and challenges that inundate you.

So, how can you make sure that you are more likely to hit your targets? I'll illustrate with this example:

You take your breathing for granted. Inhaling and exhaling is an unconscious activity that you do automatically; you don't even think about it. But if you were in a boat and it suddenly capsized, your breathing instantly goes from unconscious to very conscious – you fight for every single breath you need to take as you try to breathe while the water crashes over you. Your inner drive to breathe will make you fight with every fiber of your being.

Likewise, your targets need to be as important as oxygen. Running your business is a lot like that ocean water that crashes over you with constant problems and hassles. And your target needs to be as important as your oxygen.

When I hear of people who set New Year Resolutions and then fail to achieve them, I shake my head. I set targets and I hit more than most because I make those targets as important as oxygen – I fight with everything I have to achieve the targets that are important to me.

When Was The Last Time You Focused On Education?

Another reason why service business owners unintentionally sabotage their own businesses is because they just try to do it all themselves. They either don't realize that they need to learn something, or they belong to an industry group that might or might not teach them anything relevant.

Or another thing that happens: **service business owners know that they need to learn but they're so busy dealing with the urgent stuff that learning gets deprioritized. But that's like trying to fight a fire by only dousing the stuff that is just starting to burn without dealing with the source of the fire!**

I was the same way in those early days. I was fighting one fire after another but not taking time to learn how to deal with the main problems. As a result, my business continued to struggle even though I was working 24/7 to handle the problems.

That wake-up call of my business partner and I nearly burning out was enough to make me realize I needed to address the root of the issue, so we started getting educated.

People thought we were crazy because we spent more than $900,000 on our education over 12 years. (I know it sounds nuts but how much would you spend to have an amazing business and life?) **When I realized that education would help us address the underlying problems, it made sense to me.**

And, although $900,000 might sound like a lot of money to invest in education, I'd point out that our business today is on track to make over

$30 million this year – so $900,000 suddenly seems like a pretty damn good investment to make.

If your business feels like it's sucking, you have a choice… **you can continue fighting the small, urgent fires that keep popping up daily (those can burn up 24/7 of your time) or you can invest in your own education and build your knowledge to address the root causes – the source of the fire.**

And here's the good news: you do not need to spend $900,000 and years of your life to do it. There are ways to accelerate your education for a fraction of that investment yet still achieve the same or better results. For example, my Warrior Fast Track Academy is less than .0008 of what I invested, yet I share everything that I spent $900,000 to learn!

I'll talk about that in an upcoming chapter about "the power of proximity" and how you can get around the right people who can help you.

If your goals are not being achieved and if you want some guidance to set better targets and make those targets as important as oxygen, then you should book your free 30 minute strategy call with a Master Coach Trainer at: www.warriortoday.com

Take Action!

Recommended actions:

___ What are you tolerating in your business?

_____

_____

___ Are you ready to create massive change?

_____

_____

__ What targets will set for your business and life?

_____

_____

__ **Schedule your free 30 minute strategy call with a Master Coach Trainer at <u>www.warriortoday.com</u>**

Add your own actions:

__ Stop doing actions (Actions you currently do now but should stop doing)

_____

_____

__ Keep doing actions (Actions you currently do now and should keep doing)

_____

_____

__ Start doing actions (Actions you don't do now but should start doing)

_____

_____

__ Who will do new actions? (Assign the action to yourself or someone else)

_____

_____

___ By when? (When will these actions be complete?)

_____

_____

_____

"You either tolerate the status quo or you take action to change it. Most business owners default to tolerance and feel frustrated, when action-taking transformation creates so much freedom and fulfillment."

-Mike Agugliaro

Get the latest strategies for free at CEOWARRIOR.com…

SPECIAL REPORT:
NETWORKING YOUR WAY TO BROKE

HERE'S HOW SERVICE BUSINESS OWNERS FIND THE ONE INDUSTRY GROUP THAT WILL ACTUALLY MAKE A MEASURABLE DIFFERENCE TO THEIR BUSINESS' GROWTH... INSTEAD OF THROWING MONEY AWAY AT HIGH-COST, LOW-VALUE MEMBERSHIPS

This report is for service business owners – including plumbers, HVAC, and electricians – who understand the importance that an industry organization or group can play in the growth of their business.

If you are either currently <u>looking for an industry organization or group to join</u> or are <u>disappointed by the results you're (not) getting from the organization you currently belong to,</u> then make sure you read this report all the way through because you may be surprised by what you learn...

You're on a journey and you reach a fork in the road. But not just two potential paths... Rather, you have a dozen or more potential paths. Each path *promises* to help you get to your preferred destination but when you look at the dejected faces of people traveling in the opposite direction, you know that not every path will do what it promises.

Welcome to the world of home service industry organizations and groups. There are many available and each one promises to train you to grow your service business with the latest strategies and industry best practices, to provide networking opportunities, and perhaps discounts on marketing or services.

Unfortunately, **many service business owners learn the hard way that these organizations are not delivering on their promise; instead, they happily accept your hard-earned money for their expensive memberships but rarely deliver back the value you hope to get.**

Year after year you promise yourself, *this year I'll dig deeper to get more out of the group,* or, *this year I'll try a different group,* but you get to the end of every year and discover that nothing has changed. **Your money has been wasted.** (And yet, if you're like most service business owners, you continue in the organization because you hope that next year will bring you the value you need.")

The results speak for themselves: you might take away a half-decent idea now and then, or you might benefit from the occasional group call… but you have a hard time justifying the membership cost.

Forget the empty promises of training and networking that will once again fall through.

What do service business owners really want? If you're like most service business owners out there, you probably want **practical ideas that you can implement immediately to get fast results**; and, to be frank, **you might even benefit from the occasional get-your-ass-in-gear push to help you overcome the frustrations and obstacles that plague you daily**.

Use this list to diagnose whether you're wasting your money at your current industry organization or group, and to see what option will actually create positive measurable growth in your business.

#1. Are The Owners "In The Trenches" Every Day?

Some industry organizations and groups are run by people who haven't run a home service business in years; others are run by people who have never worked a single day in the home service industry!

CEO Warrior is owned by Mike Agugliaro and Rob Zadotti, who also own Gold Medal Service. Gold Medal Service is New Jersey's #1 home service business, employing 190 staff, serving 125,000 customers, and will earn more than $30 million this year. Mike and Rob still run their home service business and are always learning and testing to share only the strategies that have proven to work.

Would you rather hear from someone who is no longer in the business or someone who is still in the business daily?

#2. Have The Owners Of Your Industry Organization Discovered The Path To Success?

Many industry organizations simply pass down their best practices from one generation to the next, and those who run the organization just "parrot" what they've heard before. *If* they're in the industry, they're just moderately successful… or perhaps have merely *inherited* their thriving home service business rather than built it up from scratch.

Mike and Rob started out as electricians. For the first decade of their business the two of them worked 24/7 and struggled to make ends meet. After nearly burning out and shutting the business down they decided to fix what was broken, so they invested heavily in their own education then rebuilt the business from the ground up. The next eleven years were completely different, with year-over-year growth of more than a million dollars annually.

Would you rather get "hearsay advice" that is parroted from a previously successful person, or learn the strategies and systems from the same person who struggled then figured it out?

#3. Do the Owners Invest Heavily In Education?

If you currently belong to an industry organization or group, find out what the owners have learned recently. Ask them. Do they have a growing knowledgebase of current field-tested strategies that they've culled from the best-of-the-best?

CEO Warrior does! Mike and Rob have invested more than $900,000 into their education and have studied the best strategies even from organizations outside of the home service industry. Disney, Zappos, Amazon, Nordstrom, Joe Polish, and others – CEO Warrior mines the best strategies from these best-of-the-best companies.

Do you prefer stale strategies that have not been updated in years or the latest field-tested ideas inspired by the world's best-of-breed companies?

#4. Does The Industry Organization Have A Million Dollar Guarantee?

When you attend an industry event, what kind of guarantee do they have? Many don't offer any kind of guarantee; at best, you might hear the vague "If you're not satisfied, we'll try to make it right" promise.

CEO Warrior's 4-day Warrior Fast Track Academy events come with an iron-clad $1 million dollar guarantee that promises: "*If you get to the end of the very first day and you haven't learned enough strategies that will make you an extra million dollars or save you a million dollars, then simply ask for a refund and you'll get 100% of your tuition, PLUS the cost of airfare and hotel to get to the event, on the spot... no questions asked.*"

What's the guarantee of the industry event you attend?

#5. Does The Industry Organization Provide Swipe-And-Deploy Marketing Templates?

Many home service business owners fiercely protect their marketing and will never share it. That same thinking is carried over into industry organizations where you might (but probably won't) get "plain vanilla" marketing ideas that may or may not work.

CEO Warrior is different, though. You get a binder that is literally stuffed with marketing templates that are actually being used right now in the marketplace, bringing in millions of dollars of business monthly for Gold Medal Service. When you receive these marketing templates at a 4-day Warrior Fast Track Academy event, you have permission to modify and use in your own business – and you'll even be introduced to the name of the printer who can print them for you!

In your current industry group, were you handed a big swipe file and introduced to the exact people who were able to deploy it for you?

#6. Does The Industry Organization Feel Like A Brotherhood?

When you attend an industry event at your organization, what does it feel like? Do you nod silently to the other attendee before stealing a quick glance at their name tag because you can't remember who they are? You barely remember anyone's names because you just don't engage with these people enough.

At CEO Warrior, you may join the CEO Warrior Circle, which is a tight-knit brotherhood of service business owners. You'll be on a first-name basis and think of these other men and women as more than just colleagues – but as friends, family, and fellow "Warriors" as you fight together to grow your service businesses. CEO Warrior Circle members become a family and will do ANYTHING for each other, supporting each other professionally and personally.

When was the last time you felt like you were part of a close-knit brotherhood that cared about your success?

#7. Are You Just Paying For Friendships?

In most organizations, you're paying that expensive membership fee for what – a few friendships that you might or might not value outside of the networking event?

At CEO Warrior, you'll make solid friendships with other CEO Warrior Circle members but the real value of the group is the life-changing results that can transform your business and deliver more wealth, freedom, and market domination. You'll be connected to a strong group of fellow Warriors, each of whom is highly interested in your success. You'll make friends, yes, but you'll discover that the CEO Warrior Circle is all about helping you grow your business to create the business and life that you want.

Wouldn't you rather invest in yourself and your business than for expensive friendships?

#8. Do The Large Companies Just Promote Themselves?

In many industry organizations and groups, you'll encounter business owners of all sizes... And usually the small guys will chase around the big guys and try to find out what their secrets are (only to have the big guys simply promote themselves without ever sharing good ideas.)

CEO Warrior Circle is not about self-promotion but about everyone pulling together so that everyone can win. Each Warrior steps up and is willing to help the others. **What kind of brotherhood is CEO Warrior Circle? You could probably call any of them in the middle of the night for an emergency and they'd be there for you. Could you do that in your current industry organization or group?**

Would you rather hear a big company talk about themselves or a successful company share their best ideas with you?

#9. How Long Do You Have To Wait To Get Support?

One frustration that you may have with your industry organization is how long you have to wait to hear back from someone, especially if you're looking for help or advice. Maybe they only respond during business hours, or maybe they promise a 48 hour window to reply.

Mike and the CEO Warrior team are very responsive – **offering insight and advice in social posts, live video, email, and text messages at just about any time of day or night.** They recognize how important the Warriors are and they strive to serve them.

Would you rather wait hours (or days) to get help, or get help right away?

#10. Does Your Organization Take A One-Size-Fits-All Approach?

Nothing is more frustrating than getting some useful-sounding strategies... only to discover that these strategies only work in a business that is different than yours. Maybe you run a rural business but the ideas only work in town; maybe you have a team of 5 but the ideas only work if you have a team of 100.

CEO Warrior serves businesses of all sizes, in all locations. No matter how your business is configured, the strategies and guidance you'll receive will be custom-tailored to fit YOUR unique situation. There are Warriors all over the world – every size of business in many different markets. The strategies you get will work in your situation. Period.

Would you rather hear general advice that might not apply to you or the best field-tested strategies that will work in your specific situation?

#11. Is There An Emphasis On Growing Your Business Or Growing Your Life?

The last time you were at an organization or group event, how much emphasis was placed on your life? Probably very little. Most industry organizations try to help you grow your business – that's their purpose. Problem is, they don't care where you get the time and energy to make the necessary changes.

At CEO Warrior, the emphasis is on growing your business so that you can have the life you want. You'll learn the strategies to grow your business and you'll also discover how a healthy family life can help your business (and vice versa). You'll even hear how to stay healthy through the life and lifestyle of a service business owner.

Why grow your business at the expense of your family when you can have both – a successful business and a fulfilling family life?

#12. Does Your Group Tell You The Honest Truth, Even If It Hurts?

Most of us want to hear nice things – but if you're reading this then you're smart enough to know that a hurtful truth is better than a comforting lie. Yet, how often does your industry organization or group say something harsh but necessary? (Hint: they probably won't because they want you to renew your membership!)

Mike Agugliaro is known for his no holds barred, no BS approach. If a Warrior needs to hear something, Mike will say it. The honest truth, even if occasionally hurtful, is far more advantageous to hear. And, it's not just an honest truth told *to* you, there's also ongoing accountability to "hold your feet to the fire" to help you do what you say you're going to do.

If you'd rather be lied to, then join some other group. But wouldn't you rather hear the truth if it benefits you?

#13. Does Your Group "Nickel-And-Dime" You For Different Services?

In a lot of industry groups and organizations, members pay a membership fee to get access to a few things, and then they're expected to pay extra for additional products and services (like events and extra coaching).

CEO Warrior Circle members enjoy an all-inclusive experience where unlimited coaching, events, and resources are included as part of the membership investment. You simply won't get another bill for needing extra help.

Does your current group or organization care more about the fee or about you?

#14. Do You Get To Learn Directly From The Guru, Or Are You Pushed Off On Some Trainer-For-Hire?

Maybe this has happened to you: you pay your membership fee and you look forward to hearing from the guru or main person behind the group… until you actually start to interact with the group and you find out that you're stuck with a trainer-for-hire working out of a call center who follows a script and references the same resources you received when you first joined.

CEO Warrior Circle members get full access to Mike and Rob and the Master Coach Trainers – an elite group of experts who are in the industry daily. Whether by phone, text, or email (as well as webinars and events), you'll interact with the same gurus who start CEO Warrior Circle.

When was the last time you heard from the guru in your group?

#15. Do You Learn Cutting Edge Internet Marketing Strategies?

A lot of groups teach generic marketing strategies with little, if any, internet marketing. And many groups that do teach internet marketing are teaching things that worked for them 5, 10, and even 15 years ago.

CEO Warrior Circle members get the latest cutting edge internet marketing strategies that work right now for service businesses – and the reason these work is because they're being constantly tested and refined.

How current are the internet strategies you've learned? (Have you learned any? Are they currently being used?)

#16. Do They Share A Lot Of Information For Free?

Most industry groups will make a lot of promises about what you'll get when you join and force you to pay thousands of dollars to actually access the information. Very few will even give you a little glimpse into what you can learn, forcing you to put up a lot of money to find see if they're for real.

At CEO Warrior, you can learn so many strategies for free – whether by books, social media (Facebook, LinkedIn, and Twitter), or CEOWARRIOR.com, Mike shares many of his best ideas and strategies. In fact, one person watched Mike's free videos and applies his strategies over a 2-year period and increased the number of techs in his business from six to 20. And, many more business owners see even bigger results faster by attending Mike's 4-day Warrior Fast Track Academy

Could you more-than-triple your workforce from the free information provided by your industry group

#17. Do You Get A Free 30 Minute Strategy Session To Even See If This Is The Right Fit For You?

Most industry organizations and groups will tell you to pay if you want to find out whether it's right for you or not. You risk your money and time without really knowing until it's too late whether the information you're learn is helpful. Perhaps they throw some generic ideas at you in an attempt to wow you but they're just regurgitating the same information for everyone.

At CEO Warrior, no one can attend the Warrior Fast Track Academy without first getting a free 30 minute strategy session with Mike, Rob, or a Master Coach Trainer. These strategy sessions are FOR you and ABOUT the strategy, problem, question, challenge, or opportunity of YOUR choosing. Simply share the struggle you want help with and the Master Coach Trainer will work with you – for free – before you can even attend the Warrior Fast Track Academy.

When was the last time you got a 30 minute free personal one-on-one strategy session with your industry organization before they even allowed you to move forward with them?

#18. Are There Events That Your Family Wants To Attend (That Actually Help Your Family Members Understand What You Do?

Most industry events are technical and boring. Your family begs not to go, and they don't really care what you learn while you're there. But wouldn't it be nice if they could attend to understand what you do? And wouldn't it be amazing if they had such a good time that they begged to go back again?

CEO Warrior Circle members often bring their spouses to events – from regular Circle events to special Warrior Relationship events, your spouse will love the event and will have a better understanding of what you do so they can support you as you grow your business.

When was the last time you attended an event with your spouse… and your spouse asked to go back again?

#19. Do You Dread Those BORING Live Events?

Most industry events are a bore! Look around the room and you'll see people trying to stay awake while the speaker drones on and on. You keep checking your watch. You drain your coffee cup and can't wait for a break to refill it. You spend more time checking your phone for messages than you do watching another boring PowerPoint slide presentation.

CEO Warrior events, including the Warrior Fast Track Academy, are anything but boring. Audiences are captivated by Mike's style, by his strategies, and by his level of service that he brings to every presentation. Some CEO Warrior Circle events even include firewalking! Make sure you get a good night's sleep before the event because you'll be "on" the entire time, and you'll leave with a level of inspiration and energy you didn't think was possible!

When was the last time you actually were excited about attending an industry event?

#20. Do You Leave The Live Event With A Road Map Of Success?

Many people attend industry events with the hope of getting a couple of good ideas that they can bring back to their company (and sometimes they'll even remember to implement those ideas when they get back!)

But those who attend Mike Agugliaro's Warrior Fast Track Academy events get something different: you'll work WITH Mike throughout the 4-day event to create your own customized 90 Day Road Map that outlines the step-by-step strategies you want to implement in your business to grow in the next 90 days. And by the end of the event, Mike and his team will even check your Road Map to make sure it's clear and achievable so you can start implementing it immediately. (Some attendees even start implementing before they leave the event.)

When was the last time you left an industry event with a multi-million dollar step-by-step Road Map to implement in the next 90 days?

The choice is yours – will you continue paying for an industry group or organization that...

... doesn't deliver what it promises?

... takes your money and then asks for more?

... feels like an expensive way to meet a few other friends in the industry?

... is difficult to reach anybody when you need real help?

... doesn't share the best, most effective field-tested strategies and ideas?

... run by people who aren't in the industry?

... doesn't seem to care about your business (or your family)?

Or, will you finally step and realize that YOU and YOUR BUSINESS (and YOUR FAMILY) are worth making the switch to a group like CEO Warrior – a true brotherhood of like-minded business owners who want help each other, led by an industry leader who will always be there for you?

The very first step to learn more about how CEO Warrior is different is to attend the 4-day Warrior Fast Track Academy – to learn more, to get many of the benefits described above, and to see if the CEO Warrior Circle is right for you.

Go to <u>WarriorFastTrackAcademy.com</u> to apply.

SPECIAL REPORT:
HOW TO GET A VENDOR TO PAY YOU TO IMPROVE YOUR BUSINESS

Are you thinking about attending the 4-Day Warrior Fast Track Academy but you're just not sure if you can afford the financial investment right now? Maybe the money you need to invest in the Warrior Fast Track Academy is needed for some other expense.

- You've had a taste of the event or you've read some of the strategies you'll learn, and you're thinking, "Yes, I want that in my business!"
- You've heard me speak at an event or you've connected with me on social media and you know that I share everything and hold nothing back...
- You're aware of the Million Dollar Guarantee that assures you won't risk a thing when you attend...

... and yet, even while you KNOW this is the right move for you to grow your business, you're still held back by the financial investment.

I get it. I've been there. Before I transformed my business from making less than a million a year to multiple millions each year (over $30 million this year), I looked at investments like that in the same way – wondering if I could or should spend that much to learn.

So I want to share with you a very powerful strategy that will allow you to attend 4-day Warrior Fast Track Academy entirely for free (that's right, you won't spend a penny).

I call it "the **Co-op Strategy**." In our industry, vendors give co-op dollars to customers like you, and usually those dollars are earmarked for marketing. Most business owners tend to think of co-op dollars only for marketing.

However, some vendors are open to giving co-op dollars for reasons other than strictly for marketing. Have you ever thought about breaking the norms of traditional co-op dollars and asking your vendors if they would invest co-op dollars to sponsor you to come to the Warrior Fast Track Academy?

Think about it: vendor co-op dollars aren't really just to share the cost of marketing. They're really to help generate business for you and for the vendor. So when a vendor invests in your growth, they can help generate even more growth over the longer term – because the more successful you are, the more likely you'll buy more product from them. They invest... you grow... you both win. Why wouldn't your vendor want to invest in that? (And if they don't want to invest in your growth... how committed are they to your relationship?)

I used this exact strategy 7-8 years ago. I wanted to attend a high-priced, hands-on training event at the Disney Institute. Rather than cutting the check myself, I went to my vendors and told them, "Invest some co-op dollars into my training, I'll learn to grow my business, and we'll all benefit in the long-term." They invested, and I've since sent them back 1000X more than what they invested in me.

So if the Warrior Fast Track Academy seems like the best next step for you but you're hesitant on investing in yourself, apply this powerful Co-op Strategy to get your vendors to invest in you. The Co-op Strategy is a powerful way to cover the investment into your growth. Everyone wins when you apply this strategy and it's an excellent indicator to know who is really focused on your growth and success.

Think Outside The Box

I went to my vendors and told them, "You already invest in the growth of my business... when you spend co-op dollars on marketing. So invest some co-op dollars into my training, I'll learn to grow my business, and we'll all benefit in the long-term."

They invested, I got the training and grew like crazy, and I've since sent the vendors back 1000X more in orders than what they invested in me.

Make it a Win/Win

Maybe you're saying, "Okay, that's kind of a cool idea... and I'm glad it worked for you, Mike, but why would my vendors do that?"

Here's my answer...

Vendor co-op dollars aren't really just to share the cost of marketing. Vendors don't do it to be "nice guys."

Co-op dollars serve a strategic purpose that benefits the vendors: They invest co-op dollars in marketing because ultimately it generates more business for you, which, in turn, generates more business for the vendor.

Vendors aren't really interested in throwing money at marketing; they're ultimately interested in growing their businesses.

So when you approach a vendor and help them see the importance and value of your growth, and then show them how you'll grow at the Warrior Fast Track Academy, then you're accomplishing the same thing...

... you'll grow and send them more business so they'll grow.

The more successful you are, the more successful they become. When they invest co-op dollars into sending you to the Warrior Fast Track Academy, you both win.

So if the Warrior Fast Track Academy seems like the best next step for you but you're hesitant on investing in yourself, apply this powerful Co-op Strategy to get your vendors to invest in you.

Let Vendors Help You Grow

Your vendors normally share co-op dollars with you for marketing, but some vendors will spend co-op dollars on your growth, so ask them to use the co-op dollars to help you grow at my Warrior Fast Track Academy.

I used this strategy years ago to attend training, and some attendees used this same strategy at my last Warrior Fast Track Academy. It works!

It works because vendors ultimately want you to grow so that you send them more business. So instead of growing through marketing, you're growing by attending the Warrior Fast Track Academy and learning powerful strategies that can help your business grow in so many different areas – from marketing to customer service to lead generation and more.

Of course, this strategy only works if you treat your vendors like gold. You need to treat them as central to your business (they are!) and human beings (they are!) and invaluable business partners (they are!)

If you treat your vendors poorly or take them for granted, this will not work.

Steps To Put It Into Action

1. Make sure you are crystal-clear on where you're going (the Warrior Fast Track Academy), and WHY.
2. Set a meeting up with your vendors.
3. At the meeting, let them know that you appreciate them.
4. Tell them about a great opportunity to help you grow.
5. Explain why this makes sense: The larger you grow, the more you purchase from them.

When you explain it well to the right vendor, they will understand and support you. After all, people want to join and be part of changing lives, and they'll see how you can grow even more from the Warrior Fast Track Academy than you would from using their co-op dollars just to spend on marketing.

Overcoming Objections From Vendors

Maybe you approached a vendor and they said no, or maybe you haven't approached them yet because you're worried about what to do if they say no. That's okay if they say no. It happens. At least you asked and you planted the seed.

If your vendors say no, then the very next step should be for you to ask yourself the following question: "Is the vendor truly a partner and supportive of my business' growth?"

If you determine that the vendor ISN'T truly a supportive partner then you need to think about finding a different vendor who can help you. After all, if a vendor isn't willing to invest in growth then should you really be partnered with them?

If you determine that the vendor IS a supportive partner but (for whatever reason) they still didn't give you the money, then you need to figure out how you can add even more value to the relationship and prove to them that you are worth the investment. Then try again. A good vendor who is interested in your growth will likely support this kind of growth-investment.

Remember: the co-op dollars they spend on your marketing might result in a growth of "X" in the orders you send your vendor... but co-op dollars spent on your growth at the Warrior Fast Track Academy will result in a growth of "10X" or even "100X" in orders you send your vendor.

It's not unusual for attendees to leave the Warrior Fast Track Academy, implement what they've learned, and grow their business by 25%, 50%, 100%, 200%, or more... would YOUR vendor like additional orders of 25%, 50%, 100%, 200%, or more? They probably would.

Help them see the bigger benefit to them of your business growth...
... or find a vendor who can see the power of a more creative investment.

I've shared this powerful strategy with you, now it's time for you to implement. If you attend a Warrior Fast Track Academy because your vendors covered some or all of the costs, let me know! I always love hearing these success stories over and over.

Every time I hold an event, I love finding out that at least a couple attendees from each event used this strategy to invest in themselves and pay their tuition to the event. Is this the strategy for you to use to be able to attend the next Warrior Fast Track Academy?

HERE'S YOUR ACTION PLAN

I want you to succeed because of what you've read in this book. So, here is an action plan to help you move from theory and concepts into real, implementable actions.

STEP 1. Review the *Take Action* sections in each chapter and list all the actions you plan to start doing, stop doing, and keep doing. Write them into a single list, add due dates, and schedule a reminder to yourself to check on your progress. (I've provided some note-taking pages on the following pages for you.) Celebrate your progress as you go.

STEP 2. Schedule your free 30 minute strategy call with a Master Coach Trainer, and bring any problem, challenge, or opportunity to the call that you'd like help with. Schedule it here: www.warriortoday.com

STEP 3. Attend the next 4-day Warrior Fast Track Academy event and get all the systems, strategies and ideas in a swipe-and-deploy system that can transform your business like it's transformed many others.

STEP 4. Plan to join a strong industry organization or group (such as CEO Warrior Circle) that can support your journey, and as a demonstrate to your team about the importance of investing in your own personal growth.

STEP 5. Commit to transformation and take tireless action to grow your business daily. Find the balance between your growing business and enjoying the family and lifestyle you deserve. Plan to build your business so you can maybe even step away from it so it runs on autopilot while you enjoy the results of the changes you've made.

ACTION PLAN

_____

_____

_____

_____

_____

_____

_____

_____

_____

_____

_____

_____

_____

_____

_____

_____

_____

_____

_____

_____

_____

ACTION PLAN

Book your strategy call right now at www.warriortoday.com

YOU CAN DO THIS – <u>TAKE THE LEAP NOW</u>

If you're reading this then I've got good news for you: I can tell you're very serious about turning around your business from sucking to success. You can do it! I've done it and I know it's possible.

I've shared so many possibilities and strategies and ideas with you – now it's time to take action and implement those ideas.

But maybe you're thinking that you don't have quite enough yet. Or maybe you've already started implementing and you know there's more to do.

It's true, I've only been able to scratch the surface of what can be done. That's why…

The best place to make a shift in your business is by attending the Warrior Fast Track Academy.

Apply to attend at <u>WarriorFastTrackAcademy.com</u>

There is no clearer, faster way to transform your business than by learning and implementing the strategies from that 4-day event.

And **<u>NOW</u>** is the perfect time to do it. The best time to take action is immediately – that's how you'll start creating the forward momentum necessary to make change. And just think of how many opportunities you may have missed out on because you haven't attended yet… stop missing out and stop your business from sucking… get moving forward today.

Apply to attend at <u>WarriorFastTrackAcademy.com</u>

Warrior Fast Track Academy

Are you tired of treading water – staying busy in your business but never really getting ahead? Are you ready to discover the most powerful strategies to create real change, growth, and market domination in your business?

Whether you're new and totally overwhelmed or you're a seasoned pro and looking for to reignite, The Warrior Fast Track Academy can show you how to get to the next level.

Warrior Fast Track Academy is my 4-day hands-on event where I guide you and a group of like-minded service business owners through the exact plan that I used to build a $30+ million (and growing) business. I'll **reveal the blueprint and show you how you can implement the**  **same blueprint into your business**, with all areas of mastery planned out and ready to be plugged in. You'll be motivated and inspired to lead positive, profitable change in your company and take your business to never-before-seen heights.

Business owners who have attended the Warrior Fast Track Academy have said it's "life changing" and gone on to build successful businesses all around the world.

If you want to take control of your business and your future, Warrior Fast Track Academy is THE event to make that happen. To see what others are saying about Warrior Fast Track Academy, to learn more about my $1 million guarantee, and to pre-register for an upcoming event, go to <u>WarriorFastTrackAcademy.com</u>

Warrior Circle

"You are the average of the 5 people you spend the most time with." (Jim Rohn)

... Who are YOU spending time with?

Here's the fastest way to leverage the <u>power of proximity</u> by spending time with like-minded action-takers who work together – to grow your business while striving to become unstoppable.

Most industry groups and organizations take your money and give you just a few stale best practices and networking opportunities. But at CEO Warrior, we've created a powerful, exclusive "family of Warriors" who discover the best secrets and field-tested strategies, and who hold each other accountable while implementing them.

Welcome to the exclusive, invitation-only CEO Warrior Circle where business owners can join to become Warriors and inspiring leaders of a strong and growing business.

During the upcoming year, we'll revolutionize your business and your life. We'll blow your wealth, freedom and personal goals out of the water by focusing on massive business building and life strategies. From weekly calls to exclusive events, from one-on-one coaching to an exclusive vault of swipe-and-deploy resources, joining the CEO Warrior Circle gives you everything you need to grow your business.

This program is designed for action-takers who are ready to make the commitment and take action to boost their business.

To learn more about the Warrior Circle, and to see if you qualify to participate in the Mastermind, get in touch at <u>CEOwarrior.com/contact</u> .

Read The Free Magazine Written For The Home Service Industry

Discover new information, insight, and industry-specific success stories in **Home ServiceMAX** – the free online magazine written for home service business owners.

Each issue of Home ServiceMAX is packed with practical tips and strategies that you can implement right away into your home service business. They're field-tested and written by experts and industry insiders.

Home ServiceMAX will help you improve your sales, marketing, finance, human resources and customer service. Keep it on hand as you develop best practices to meet your team's unique challenges.

Whether you're a plumber, electrician, carpenter, roofer, builder, painter or specialist in any other service industry trade, to survive you must also stand out as a business leader. We designed this magazine to help you achieve that goal.

Each easy-to-read issue is available online for free. Check out the articles and make sure you have a pen and paper in hand to write down all the actions you'll want to take when you're done each article.

Read the current issue and subscribe here: **HomeServiceMaxMag.com** .

ABOUT THE AUTHOR

Mike Agugliaro
Business Warrior

Mike Agugliaro helps his clients grow their service businesses utilizing his $30 Million Warrior Fast Track Academy Blueprint, which teaches them how to achieve massive wealth and market domination.

Two decades ago, he founded Gold Medal Electric with his business partner Rob. After nearly burning out, he and Rob made a change: they developed a powerful blueprint that grew the company. Today, Gold Medal Service is now the top service industry provider in Central New Jersey. With over 190 staff and 140 trucks on the road, Gold Medal Service now earns over $30 million in revenue each year.

Mike is a transformer who helps service business owners and other entrepreneurs master themselves and their businesses, take control of their dreams and choices, and accelerate their life and business growth to new heights. Mike is the author of the popular book *The Secrets Of Business Mastery*, in which he reveals 12 areas that all service business owners need to master.

Mike speaks and transforms around the world; his Warrior Fast Track Academy events are popular, transformational events for service business owners; he also leads a mastermind of business owners known as Warrior Circle. Mike has been featured in MSNBC, Financial Times, MoneyShow, CEO World, and more.

Mike is an avid martial artist who has studied karate, weaponry, jujitsu, and has even developed his own martial art and teaches it to others. The discipline of martial arts equips him to see and act on opportunities, create change in himself and others, and see that change through to successful completion.

Mike is a licensed electrician and electrical inspector, he is a certified Master Fire Walk Instructor, certified professional speaker, and a licensed practitioner of Neuro-Linguistic Programming (NLP).

Whether firewalking, breaking arrows on his neck, studying martial arts, transforming businesses, or running his own business, Mike Agugliaro leads by powerful example and is changing the lives and businesses of service business owners everywhere.

Mike lives in New Jersey with his wife and two children.

IN THE MEDIA

An article published in the HVACR Business Magazine discussing the struggles of being a service business owner and sharing his Situation Analysis Tool to help make better business decisions.

READ

ceowarrior.com/hvacr

This article is about strategies to build a strong and productive team. This is one of many articles that Mike has published through Comfortech.

READ

ceowarrior.com/contractor

Featured in a TV segment on the Nightly Business Report on CNBC. This interview shares how Mike, as an electrician, started his own business and is now advising other entrepreneurs how to be a CEO Warrior in their business.

WATCH

ceowarrior.com/cnbc

CEOWORLD MAGAZINE

5 Mindset Shifts To Rapidly Grow Your Business

Mike shares 5 powerful mindset shifts to rapidly grow your business. These are some that helped him grow his $28M business.

READ

ceowarrior.com/ceoworld

IN THE MEDIA

Mike shares tips on how to motivate your staff by discovering their why. It's a strategy he uses to leverage and motivate his staff of 190 with great success.

READ

ceowarrior.com/thenews

Vendors are a great resource – and Mike explains why. He explains how you should choose your vendors to create stronger and more lucrative relationships and partnerships. This article was also published in Entrepreneur!

WATCH

ceowarrior.com/foxnews

MSNBC interviews Mike Agugliaro and business partner Rob Zadotti to share how they grew their service business from $1M a year to over $28M one employee at a time, through processes and systems.

READ

ceowarrior.com/msnbc

CBS8 featured an article about Mike, CEO Warrior and the 4 Day Warrior Fast Track Academy and how it helps service business owners.

READ

ceowarrior.com/cbs8

READ MIKE'S BOOKS

The Secrets Of Business Mastery: Build Wealth, Freedom and Market Domination For Your Service Business in 12 Months or Less. A chapter-by-chapter collection of best business practices, tools and strategies for service business owners.

Secrets of Leadership Mastery: 22 Powerful Keys To Unlock Your Team's Potential and Get Better Results: 22 powerful keys to help you create a culture where you build and lead a hardworking team of superstars, inspire them to give their very best, and generate measurable results.

Secrets of Communication Mastery: 18 Laser Focused Tactics To Communicate More Effectively. We all communicate. We can all learn to communicate more effectively. When you do, you'll see instant results in every personal and professional relationship.

Timeless Secrets of A Warrior. Discover the most powerful, time-tested Warrior secrets that will propel you toward success by revealing strategies from some of history's greatest minds.

9 Pillars Of Business Mastery Program: Discover the nine most powerful and transformative strategies that are PROVEN to completely transform your business and your life.

CONNECT WITH MIKE AGUGLIARO

Connect with Mike in the following places and find even more free resources and strategies to help you grow your business.

Website: **CEOwarrior.com** – Go here now to get free resources, including chapters from Mike's book and a library of resources.

Podcast: **CEOwarrior.com/podcast**

Events: **CEOwarrior.com/events**

Social: Visit **CEOwarrior.com** to connect with Mike on Facebook, Twitter, LinkedIn, and elsewhere.

Home ServiceMAX Magazine: **HomeServiceMaxMag.com**

TAKE ACTION NOW – GET THE WARRIOR LIBRARY

Want a **free** bundle of strategies, tools, and resources that I use daily in my $30+ million service business? The **Warrior Library** contains powerful strategies to help you achieve wealth, freedom, and market domination.

Get them at: www.CEOWARRIOR.com/warriorlibrary

Made in the USA
Columbia, SC
01 September 2019